GREAT DOCTRINES OF THE BIBLE

W.A.Criswell

GREAT DOCTRINES OF THE BIBLE

Volume 2 ○ Theology Proper/ Christology

Edited by
Paige Patterson, President
Criswell Center for Biblical Studies

ZONDERVAN
PUBLISHING HOUSE   OF THE ZONDERVAN CORPORATION
GRAND RAPIDS, MICHIGAN 49506

GREAT DOCTRINES OF THE BIBLE, Volume 2
Copyright © 1982 by The Zondervan Corporation
Grand Rapids, Michigan

Library of Congress Cataloging in Publication Data

Criswell, W. A. (Wallie A.), 1909–
    Great doctrines of the Bible.

    1. Bible—Sermons. 2. Baptists—Sermons. 3. Sermons, American. I. Patterson,
Paige. II. Title.
BS491.5.C73   1982   252'.0613   81-16334
ISBN 0-310-43860-8 (v. 2)

First printing September 1982

Edited by Paige Patterson

Printed in the United States of America

Dedication

With abiding love and growing appreciation, I dedicate this second volume of doctrinal sermons to Mr. and Mrs. Horace Pritchett. Evalee serves as my administrative assistant and unselfishly gives of her time and energies in the work of the kingdom. Horace, her godly deacon husband, has been wonderfully understanding of the long and copious hours of her labor for our dear church.

Contents

Foreword

This series of doctrinal sermons represents the climax of many years of preaching and writing. The first volume established the foundation upon which all that follows must be built. I have given more hours in research and more time in study and meditation to the preparation of these messages than to any other series I have presented in my more than fifty years of preaching. It is my earnest prayer that all of these volumes will provide for the reader a clear understanding of the truths of Scripture concerning the great doctrines of our faith. They are presented in these pages, not as professional, academic lectures in a classroom, but as an appeal for souls from a pulpit to a living congregation.

Many have assisted me in this project. Certainly I am deeply indebted to the president of our Center for Biblical Studies, Dr. Paige Patterson. This gifted and learned theologian assumed the responsibility for overseeing the task of editing these many sermons that will extend over a several-year period of pulpit ministry. The typist for this project is the very efficient and capable Jo Ellen Burch, and the stylistic editing has been done by Dr. Dorothy Patterson. Then, last but not least, I owe a debt of gratitude to the layman in our great church who made the project possible by providing equipment and secretary. He insists on remaining anonymous to you, but God has recorded his deed of kindness.

W. A. Criswell
Pastor's Study
First Baptist Church
Dallas, Texas

Introduction

This volume contains no ivory-tower theology. The research has been thorough as if the author wished to present an erudite, multi-volume *Magnum Opus*. Then the research was laid before the One whose eyes are "like a flame of fire" until cold insights were warmed into white-hot convictions of the soul in prayer before God.

Then, twice each Lord's day morning, Dr. W. A. Criswell approached the sacred desk in the auditorium of the First Baptist Church in Dallas, Texas, where he has served as pastor for thirty-seven years. Three thousand people, a standing-room-only crowd, lined the holy place in the heart of one of America's great cities, and listened intently as the investigations, experiences, and convictions of a fifty-year ministry resounded throughout the sanctuary.

Nor were these concepts laboriously deposited in the minds of hearers gathered for the purpose of curing the most hopeless insomniac. Those of us who attended each Sunday went like "empty pitchers to a full fountain." We listened to profound truths depicted in picturesque language, cogently illustrated, and delivered with the fiery oratorical excellence that has characterized our pastor from his youth. We laughed, wept, confessed, expressed thanksgiving, and marched out to engage the enemy.

Each volume of doctrinal sermons represents theology propounded where it ought to be—in the congregation of the Lord. The initial volume concentrated on bibliology, the doctrine of the believer's source of authority for faith and practice. This second volume is devoted to the doctrine of Theology proper and Christology. Subsequent volumes in the series will encompass pneumatology, ecclesiology, eschatology, and others.

We wish to express our special gratitude to Dr. Criswell's friend of many years, Mr. Pat Zondervan, who encouraged the pastor to produce sermonically his mature theological reflection.

In the hope that it will bless the Christian world as greatly as it has blessed our dear church, we humbly present Dr. W. A. Criswell's sermons on the great doctrines of the faith.

Paige Patterson, President
Criswell Center for Biblical Studies

GREAT
DOCTRINES
OF
THE
BIBLE

1

God and the Reasoning Mind

One of the characteristics of the apostle Paul, as observed by Dr. Luke who worked with him, watched him, journeyed by his side, and then wrote of him in the Book of Acts, is that he reasons. Paul reasoned in the Agora, in the marketplace, in the synagogue, and even as he stood before the Roman procurator Felix. For example, we read in Acts 17:1–3:

> Now when they had passed through Amphipolis and Apollonia, they came to Thessalonica, where was a synagogue of the Jews:
> And Paul, as his manner was, went in unto them, and three sabbath days reasoned with them out of the scriptures,
> Opening and alleging, that Christ must needs have suffered, and risen again from the dead. . . .

Notice that descriptive clause, he "reasoned with them out of the scriptures."

We read in Acts 18:

> After these things Paul departed from Athens, and came to Corinth;
> And he reasoned in the synagogue every sabbath, and persuaded the Jews and the Greeks.
> And he came to Ephesus, and left them there: but he himself entered into the synagogue, and reasoned with the Jews (Acts 18:1, 4, 19).

Now turn to Acts 24:

> And after certain days, when Felix came with his wife Drusilla, which was a Jewess, he sent for Paul, and heard him concerning the faith in Christ.

> And as he reasoned of righteousness, temperance, and judg-
> ment to come, Felix trembled, and answered, Go thy way for this
> time; when I have a convenient season, I will call for thee (Acts
> 24:24–25).

What did Felix think he would hear when he called for the
apostle Paul? Would it be an unimaginable, unlikely portrayal of
what some superstitious mind might be able to describe? The
Scripture says that Paul reasoned of righteousness, temperance,
and judgment to come.

WHY DO WE SEEK ANSWERS?

It is the way we are made that makes us seek an answer.
Plato, concerning Greek rationality, gave us this statement, "A
man must attempt to give an account of things because he is a
man, not merely because he is Greek." The characteristic of the
Greek was to probe, to inquire, but Plato observes that this
philosophical bent was not just a characteristic of the Greek but
also a characteristic of any man. Our hearts seek and demand an
answer. Not only is it characteristic of us to seek satisfying answers, but also when others ask questions of us, we ought to
have an answer ready for them (cf. 1 Peter 3:15).

It is not right to sneer at the arguments and questions of the
humanists, the materialists, the secularists, the infidels, or the
atheists. We ought to answer them. Nor is it right for us to ignore
those in our midst who have doubts and questions. People are
surprised to learn that sometimes even I, a pastor and teacher for
half a century, am overwhelmed by doubt and must seek an answer in the mind of God. This is not contrary to the will of our
Lord. Simon Peter wrote in his first epistle,

> But sanctify the Lord God in your hearts: and be ready always
> to give an answer to every man that asketh you a reason of the hope
> that is in you with meekness and fear (1 Peter 3:15).

All of you are familiar with that third verse of Jude in which
the writer urges us to "earnestly contend" (*epagonizesthai*) for
the faith. We are to plead, not peripherally, indifferently, or su-
perficially, but agonizingly so. This seeking an answer that is ra-
tional, intelligent, and acceptable is in the will of God.

God made us free in our minds, hearts, wills, and souls. He
did that in the beginning with our first parents. Out of all that lay
before them, they had choice, freedom of spirit and will. That

freedom of mind and soul cannot be denied us. We can coerce, imprison, incarcerate a body, but we cannot imprison a mind. There is a part of a hymn that says,

> Our fathers chained in prisons dark
> Were still in mind and conscience free.

My body may be imprisoned, but my mind is free! What a powerful weapon, therefore, God gives us in persuasion—not in coercion, but in reasoning. If I can win a man's mind and heart, I have the whole man. That is why God addresses His gospel message to the mind, the heart, and the soul. God is truth and He revealed Himself in John 1:1 as the Logos. What is the Logos? It is the reason of God, the mind of God, the intelligence of God, the thought of God. John 1:1 comprises the most astounding of all the philosophical sentences in human literature. "In the beginning was the Word," . . . the reason, the mind, the intelligent activity of God. Reason was face to face with God and God was reason and mind. It is an amazing and marvelous thing when you look carefully, not superstitiously, sneeringly, or with ridicule, at the Word of God to see that our blessed Lord addresses His message to the intelligence of the man. Look, see, handle, judge for yourself. It is an intelligent and reasonable gospel, and it is reasonable to be a Christian.

THE WITNESS TO THE INTELLECTUAL WORLD

We now come to Paul's address in Athens, a city that was renowned as the university center of all of the ancient world. He stood before the Areopagus, i.e., the Supreme Court of Attica, in the capital city of Athens. He stood before those learned and gifted Athenians. There has never been sculpture, drama, literature, poetry, or philosophy that can excel what was done by the Greeks, and the science that we know today is just an extension of what they discovered years ago. Paul stood in the midst of that university center and delivered his reasoning and reasonable address. As he stood before the people, one group to which he spoke included the pagan polytheists. They had no trouble accepting what they called the "new gods," about whom Paul was preaching.

As Paul stood before them, they were enticed by his preaching concerning these "new gods" because Paul preached *Jesus*

17

(in Greek, a masculine form that could suggest a male deity) and *anastasis* (in Greek, a feminine form that could suggest a female deity). Paul preached "Jesus" and the "resurrection." The Athenians had been acquainted all their lives with pairs of gods. There were many couples: Jupiter (Jove) and Juno, Isis and Osiris, etc. So when Paul spoke, they were intrigued by Jesus and *anastasis,* whom they assumed to be a pair of new gods. They would have added Jesus and *anastasis* to Jove and Juno, Isis and Osiris. However, Paul preached that they should not think of the godhead in pairs, represented by gold or silver or stone graven by art and man's device. Paul said that God in the past had overlooked this misunderstanding because of the lack of knowledge of the people, but now He commands all men everywhere to turn to the Truth. The pagan polytheists in the crowd to which Paul was preaching refused to accept the exclusiveness of Jesus alone as the one true and living God.

The other group to whom Paul spoke in Athens was an altogether different kind. They were the philosophers who, like us, scoffed at gods made out of stone and wood graven by man's device. All of those mythological characters that were supposed to live on Mount Olympus, such as are described in Homer's *Iliad* and *Odyssey* and in all of the dramatic literature of Euripides, Aristophanes, and Sophocles, were viewed as idiocy to them, just as they are to you and me. Those philosophers to whom Paul was preaching were materialists of the first order, and they were atheists of the deepest stripe and color. They were materialistic atheists, and they were atheistic materialists. Two of the groups are named in Acts 17:18,

> Then certain philosophers of the Epicureans, and of the Stoics, encountered him. And some said, What will this babbler [*spermologos* or "seed-picker"] say? other some, He seemeth to be a setter forth of strange gods: because he preached unto them Jesus and the resurrection.

This is an interesting confrontation between the apostle Paul and these university men, the most learned of the age, i.e., the Epicureans and the Stoics.

Long ago there was a Greek philosopher named Democritus, who died in 370 B.C. He propounded a theory of the universe that is compelling indeed. In Greek the word *temno* means "to cut." *Tomos,* an adjectival form of it, means "cutable" or "divisible." An alpha privative added to the front of it, *a tomos* or "atom" changes the meaning to "uncutable," "indivisible." Democritus propounded the philosophical explanation of what we see as being this: Everything is made out of atoms, whirling, jostling particles that differ only in size, weight, and refinement. He taught that the finer atoms made up the soul of a man, and the coarser atoms made up the material world around us. In life the atoms came together; in death, they are dissolved and scattered. Thus, they combined in living form and then lost their combination in death. The whole universe is made up of these "uncutable," "indivisible" particles that Democritus called *a tomos*.

Epicurus, who died in 270 B.C., exactly one hundred years after Democritus, took that materialistic philosophy of Democritus and propounded his world view upon it. All life is nothing but a gathering together of atoms; it has no meaning and no purpose. Therefore, Epicurus taught that we ought to get the most we can out of the brief span of our lives. Be happy, be joyful, get all the pleasure you can wring out of it. The famous sentence, "Eat, drink, and be merry, for tomorrow we die," is the philosophy of Epicurus.

Zeno, who died about six years after Epicurus, was no less a materialist and atheist. Zeno taught on the *stoa*, the "porch." Those who attended his philosophical school came to be known as the Stoics. Zeno taught that God is the world and the world is God. He was a pure pantheist. Pantheism declares that the whole universe is God. Out of that philosophical foundation, Zeno drew the conclusion that the highest joy and privilege of the man is to yield himself to the providences of life. Do not fight against them; accept them. From this we get the word "stoical." The man who accepts any providence in life is "stoical," unmoved; he has the virtue of fortitude. The basic teaching of Zeno and his Stoics and Epicurus and his Epicureans is always materialistic and atheistic.

THE WITNESS OF THE HUMAN HEART

Paul, standing before those university men and the polytheists gathered around them, preached a message of an altogether different character and kind. Paul spoke of a personal, living God whom we can know, feel, touch, worship, adore, and serve. As Paul presented his message then, he first of all declared a universal truth: The human heart witnesses to the reality of a personal and living God.

> For as I passed by, and beheld your devotions, I found an altar with this inscription, TO THE UNKNOWN GOD, whom therefore ye ignorantly worship, him declare I unto you.
>
> God that made the world and all things therein, seeing that he is Lord of heaven and earth, dwelleth not in temples made with hands;
>
> Neither is worshiped with men's hands, as though he needed any thing, seeing he giveth to all life, and breath, and all things;
>
> And hath made of one blood all nations of men for to dwell on all the face of the earth, and hath determined the times before appointed, and the bounds of their habitation;
>
> That they should seek the Lord, if haply they might feel after him, and find him, though he be not far from every one of us:
>
> For in him we live, and move, and have our being; as certain also of your own poets have said, For we are also his offspring.
>
> Forasmuch then as we are the offspring of God, we ought not to think that the Godhead is like unto gold, or silver, or stone, graven by art and man's device (Acts 17:23–29).

He preached of a God who is nearby, who is close, who has placed in our hearts a desire to seek Him and to find Him. All of the philosophies of the world cannot stifle the instinctive hunger and cry of the human heart for God. It is a universal appeal.

Recently I read again Augustine's *Confessions.* In the first paragraph is a sentence that I have heard quoted so often, "O, God, thou hast made us for Thyself, and we are restless until we rest in Thee." There is a universal hunger for God that we cannot drown or stifle.

The late Will Durant, formerly chairman of the philosophy department at Columbia University and author of the famous volume *Story of Philosophy* wrote,

> God who was once the consolation of our brief life, and our refuge in bereavement and suffering has apparently vanished from the scene; no telescope, no microscope discovers him. Life has become in that total perspective which is philosophy, a fitful pullulation of human insects on the earth; nothing is certain in it except defeat and death—a sleep from which, it seems there is no awakening. . . . Faith and hope disappear; doubt and despair are the order of the day. . . . It seems impossible any longer to believe in the permanent greatness of man, or to give life a meaning that cannot be annulled by death. . . . The greatest question of our time is not communism vs. individualism, not Europe vs. America, not even East vs. West; it is whether man can bear to live without God.

Universally, there is a distinctive cry in the human heart for God. All of the advancement we have made and all the tools and gadgetry of science that we command do not change it. All the coercive power of a government like communist Russia is not able to crush it out. This seeking and longing and searching after God stays in our hearts forever!

Is it possible that we have that longing in our hearts for God, only to be mocked and ridiculed and derided? Is it there to crush us and to bow us into the dust in defeat and agony? If that is why it is there, that is the only instance in God's universe without an intelligent reason, purpose, and design back of it.

For example, if the earth, swinging around the sun, swung in its path just a little slower, it would be pulled by gravity into the sun. As it goes around the earth, if it were just a little faster, it would lose its orbit and would be flung into space. The design is perfect and it swings just right. If our earth were just a little nearer the sun, we would burn up. If it were just a little further from the sun, we would freeze to death. The whole universe has purpose and design. The fin of a fish has a purpose. The wing of a bird is designed for a reason. The hoof of a horse is made for a purpose. The hand of a man in its marvelous design has a purpose. God placed in our souls a hunger for Him, and He did it with design, reason, and purpose. Paul says the desire for God is in our souls that we might seek the Lord, that we might find Him, for in Him we live and move and have our being.

THE WITNESS OF THE MARVELOUS REALITY OF CHRIST

The greatest of all the confirmations of the existence and reality of the Almighty is the revelation of God in Christ Jesus. "He that hath seen me, hath seen the Father" (John 14:9). Christ is the knowable God, the touchable God, the living God, the incarnate God, Jesus our Lord.

The one great incontrovertible fact of all time and creation is Jesus our Lord. The world cannot bury Him, the earth is not deep enough for His tomb, the clouds are not wide enough for His winding sheet, and the rocks are not big enough to cover His grave. He arose, He lives, He ascended into heaven, but the heaven of heavens cannot contain Him. He lives like a bush burning unconsumed in His churches and in our hearts. He stands uppermost in human history, in the life of the ages.

21

Like some great, towering mountain, Jesus looms in the
earth, the farther slope reaching back to the Creation and the
beginning of time, and the nearer slope reaching toward the great
consummation of the ages. The eyes of those in the days past
look forward to Him with prophetic gaze, and we in this generation look back to Him in historic faith. He stands in the center of
history. Before Him, it was B.C., before Christ; after Him it is A.D.
anno Domini, in the year of our Lord. The very place where He
was born and died is the center of the universe. All of the nations
in the West write and read from left to right toward Him, and all
of the cultures and nations in the East read and write from right
to left, centering in Him. He is the manifestation of God.

> . . . [He] is the image of the invisible God . . . (Col. 1:15).

> In him dwelleth all the fullness of the Godhead bodily (Col.
> 2:9).

> [He is] the brightness of his glory, and the express image of his
> person . . . (Heb. 1:3).

> . . . He that hath seen me hath seen the Father . . . (John 14:9).

To know Jesus is to know God; to love Jesus is to love God;
to worship Jesus is to worship God; to bow before Jesus is to
bow before God. He is the knowable and touchable God to
youth, to men and women in their strength, to those nearing
death and seeking the touch of a hand on the other side. He is to
us the manifestation of the personal God. The fullness of the
revelation of God is found in Him.

Paul wrote in 2 Corinthians 4:6,

> For God, who commanded the light to shine out of darkness,
> hath shined in our hearts, to give the light of the knowledge of the
> glory of God in the face of Jesus Christ.

When God would give the light of the knowledge of His
glory to men, how did He proceed and to what did He direct our
gaze? To the universe around us? No, though that proclaims the
glory of the Lord. To the providences of life where He presides
over history? No, though He weighs the nations like fine dust in a
balance. To the astronomical stars that shine above us? No! He
guides us to the face of Jesus Christ. The tears of Jesus are the
pity of God, the gentleness of Jesus is the long-suffering of God,
and the tenderness of Jesus is the love of God.

22

God and the Reasoning Mind

It was Thomas, looking upon our risen and glorified Lord, who said, "My Lord, and my God!"

It was John who wrote,

> And when I saw him, I fell at his feet as dead. And he laid his right hand upon me, saying unto me, Fear not; I am the first and the last:
>
> I am he that liveth, and was dead; and, behold, I am alive for evermore, Amen; and have the keys of hell and of death (Rev. 1:17–18).

He is our Lord and our God! God and the reasoning mind—this truth is not strange or far out, but reasonable, intelligently so. It is right. To accept Jesus Christ as Savior and Lord fits and completes truth in both heaven and earth.

2

God, the First Universal Fact

In the beginning God. . . . (Gen. 1:1).

What happened in the beginning? The sages of ancient Egypt said that a cosmic egg was made from the mud of the Nile River. The ancient Chaldeans declared that the world began with the flattened body of the monster Tiamat, slain by Marduk. According to a hymn of the *Rigveda,* the sacred scriptures of the Hindu, the world began with the dissevered limb of a monstrous giant.

In modern times, the evolutionist says that the world began by blind, impersonal, accidental chance. The humanist and the secular physicist suggest that the world began with the exploding and hurling through space of a ball of fire. But, according to the Holy Scriptures, it was "In the beginning, God!"

THE IDEA OF GOD IS UNIVERSAL TO THE HUMAN MIND

The idea of God is innate, intuitive, congenital, and universal to the human mind. In the first chapter of Romans, as Paul is laying the groundwork for his great theological treatise, he avows that the idea of God is universally revealed in every human heart. Experience dictates affirmation of that scriptural truth.

Helen Keller was blind, deaf, and dumb. The only avenue of contact through which she could be reached was the sense of touch. When finally, through that sense, her teacher reached her, she told Helen Keller about God. And Helen replied, "I have known Him all the days of my life."

There are certain great truths that are ingrained and grounded in human personality and in the reasoning mind, and they cannot be obviated or discarded or denied. These common truths are self-evident. They belong to the recognitive faculties of our structural make-up. For example, there is no effect without a cause: a hole is greater than any one of its parts; the shortest distance between two points is a straight line. In the maxims of mathematics, $2 + 2 = 4$. These common truths are congenital with us; they are intuitive; they need no defense.

The universe everywhere and in all of its parts gives beautiful and eloquent evidence of law, of design, and of intelligence. The human personality is morally sensitive. These common truths cannot be denied. Therefore, from where did the law, the design, the intelligence in the marvelous world about us come? Who created human personality and moral religious sensitivity? What is its source?

There are those—the secularist, the evolutionist, the atheist, the humanist, the materialist—who avow that this common denominator of all mankind, which is grounded in the very personality of human life itself, is without cause, reason, reality, or fact. They say it is a blind, accidental phenomenon. For the most part, they persuade the academic world of their hypothetical, theorizing views. It is strange that even with all of their efforts, they cannot discard the idea of God from the human race and the human mind. Sometimes I think of their efforts as I would a man who pulls a plumb line horizontal. He lets the bob loose, and immediately it assumes its original vertical position. So it is with the human mind. It can be warped and twisted into all kinds of abnormalities and absurdities, but if you let it go, it will immediately assume its former position and be straight up and down, pointing to God.

There are certain phenomena and truths that are all around us, each one of which demands an explanation. Here is one: All humanity has a sense of infinitude, an impression of the glory and wonder of the chalice of the sky above us, and the marvel of the verdant earth upon which we live. There is in us a sense of the infinite, and that sense is empty, vague, and void unless it is filled with the reality and the presence of God. Our sense of the infinite presupposes a great and omnipotent creator God. It is as our eye. The eye presupposes light by which it can see. Our ear presupposes sound by which it can hear. Our sense of touch presupposes tangible objects. Our affinities and affections for one another presuppose someone to love. Our thirst presupposes water to drink. Our hunger presupposes food to eat. So our aspirations, our moral sensitivities, our religious feelings presuppose something over and above and beyond the material substance of matter. Matter calls for a creator; a creator calls for intelligence; intelligence calls for personality; personality calls for God.

When we look at the infinitude around us and the glory above, beyond, in, through, and beneath us, we know that whoever did it was a master workman! There is no such thing as a masterpiece without the intelligence of a master workman. It took a master workman to write Homer's *Iliad* or Virgil's *Aeneid* or Dante's *Divine Comedy* or Shakespeare's *Hamlet* or John Milton's *Paradise Lost.* It took a master mind to draw Raphael's *Sistine Madonna* or Michelangelo's *The Last Judgment.* It took a master workman to compose Beethoven's Fifth Symphony. It took a master workman to create the great pieces of statuary that we see adorning the glorious museums of the world. It took a master workman to create Alexander the Great's Greek empire. Shall we then deny the fact that it also took a master workman to create the glories of the world that we see above and around us?

Here is another fact that demands an explanation. In this world of creation, universally we find intelligence, mind, choice, purpose. A little boy was seated at a dinner table. The illustrious guest of his family was a professor of physics. As the adults talked, the little fellow tried to enter into the conversation as best he could. The conversation finally revolved around the world and the things that are in it as would be a natural subject for a physicist. So as a little boy would, he made the observation that there are millions of things in the world. The professor said, "No, son. In the whole world there are only 103 different things." "Oh," said the boy, "I know millions of them myself." The professor said, "Well, name some of them, son." The lad looked at the table and said, "Salt." The professor said, "Son, salt is made up of two things: it has a little piece of white metal called sodium and a little piece of gas called chlorine. Together these two elements make salt." The boy said, "Water." The professor replied: "Water is two things: two little tiny pieces of hydrogen, and one tiny piece of oxygen. Together they make water." The lad tried again, "Air." The professor replied, "Air is made of three things: seventy-nine tiny pieces of nitrogen, twenty-one tiny pieces of oxygen, and one little trace of carbonic acid or carbon dioxide. A combination of these elements over the world makes the same thing—air." The whole world, together with all that is in it, is composed of 103 different things—plus intelligence!

It is like mathematics. Mathematics has ten elements: 1, 2, 3, 4, 5, 6, 7, 8, 9, and 0. Out of those ten factors, an intelligent mind can solve problems in algebra, geometry, trigonometry, or calculus.

The world of literature contains in our language twenty-six factors or letters of the alphabet. Intelligence can take those twenty-six factors and create a literary masterpiece such as Psalm 23, the Gettysburg Address, or any of the beautiful poetry and literature of the world.

In the field of music, an octave on the keyboard contains eight notes, which are then repeated. The black notes are placed by twos and threes. When you count them all, there are twelve different notes. Those twelve notes, governed by an intelligent being, can create the beautiful music that we hear.

Thus, God took 103 elements and created in His infinite design and intelligence, the marvelous world that we see around us. The atheist, the infidel, the secularist, and the humanist say that all of this came to pass by blind chance. They are deeply committed to that thesis, and they teach it in the schools of our land!

When I can see the ten factors of mathematics thrown up into the air and have them accidentally come down as the solution to a problem in algebra or trigonometry or calculus, I will believe that hypothetical theory. I will believe it when I can see someone take the twenty-six factors of the alphabet and throw them up into the air so that they come down accidentally as one of the great masterpieces of Alfred Lord Tennyson. I will believe that theory when I see someone take twelve musical notes and throw them up into the air so that they come down as Richard Wagner's *Bridal Chorus*. I will believe it when I see an explosion in a printing plant accidentally produce an unabridged dictionary. Purposeless, accidental providences create nothing!

There is a law in thermodynamics called entropy. The law of entropy is this: If anything begins to disarray, it has a tendency to become more and more disarrayed. If the engine in your automobile starts missing and having trouble, unless it is corrected, it will become increasingly worse. All things in the universe are like that. If a thing has a tendency to fall into disarray, it will continue in that tendency unless there is intelligence to intervene. So it is in everything that we see. If you take the words from Alfred Tennyson's "Crossing the Bar" and throw them up in the air, when they come down there may be one or two little lines still intact. You throw it up again and those one or two little lines will become more disarrayed. If you keep throwing it up, it will lose all its semblance to the beautiful poetry that the author wrote. Without intelligence the whole spectrum of creation would fall into chaos! It is intelligence that brings it to order, to symmetry, to purpose, and to design. Without that, it is darkness and chaos. As the Scripture says, "The Spirit of God moved upon the face of the waters, and God said. . . ." And by that act He created the wonderful world in which we live.

Whenever I see 103 elements assemble themselves out of nothing and create without design a jet that can take off and fly into the wild, blue yonder, I am quite ready to be a secular atheist and an evolutionary physicist! I will be an evolutionist and believe in accidental, blind chance when I see a bridge cross a great chasm without an engineer or when I hear a beautiful piece of music without a composer or when I read a marvelous poem without an author or when I see a plain, simple dress made without a designer. It is the intelligent purpose that lies behind the creation of these factors that makes our world possible.

The Daily Miraculous Intervention of God

Let us look at the marvelous hand of the intervening God around us in our everyday life. There is a law of physics. This law says that when anything is heated, it expands; when anything is cooled, it contracts—the little molecules all huddle together. We experience that all the time. When we get hot, we expand, we take off our clothes, we stretch out, we do everything we can to get cool; when it gets cold, we contract, we huddle up in a little knot. All creation is like that. When a thing is heated, it expands—anything, everything, even a piece of steel.

When the bridge across the Mississippi River at Memphis was being built, it was done in the hot summer. The steel had so expanded that when the builders tried to set down the central span, it was about eighteen inches too long. What did they do? They brought in tons and tons of ice and cooled it down! Then they could set it in place perfectly. It had contracted. This illustrates a universal fact—i.e., until the intervention of God.

Water, when it cools, contracts until it gets to 32° F., and then in the intervention of God, suddenly and without reason or explanation, it expands! If it did not expand at 32°, if it would keep on contracting, it would turn to solid ice and sink like a stone to the bottom of the ocean. You would have great seas of ice at the Poles, and all of the life-giving currents of the oceans and the seas would stop, and the world would die! Such is God's power!

Consider the world of biology. The law of biology is this: In every flesh there are a certain number of chromosomes, and in every cell in that flesh there are the same number of chromosomes. The chicken, monkey, dog, cow—every cell in each one of them has a certain number of chromosomes. I remember that the drosophila with which they have been experimenting for a hundred years has two chromosomes. As for us, the human male and female, in every cell of our bodies we have forty-six chromosomes. We are made up of trillions of cells, and in every one of them we have forty-six chromosomes. Then comes the intervention of God, the miracle of God. In the male spermatozoon there are twenty-three chromosomes, and in the female ovum there are twenty-three chromosomes, and when they come together, we have a miraculous creation of God with just the right number of chromosomes—i.e., forty-six. That is why when a baby is dedicated before the Lord in our church, I cannot help but always pray, "Lord, Lord, we are grateful for the miraculous hand that shaped this little life and gave it breath and soul and lent the little child to us."

Consider again the world beneath us. It is a law of pathology that disease multiplies and extends itself. It goes on a rampage. It becomes epidemic. Germs multiply. The world is a vast cemetery. It is a burying place. Think of the germs of diptheria, polio, typhoid, scarlet fever, tetanus. Think of the diseases that are buried in the earth! There are dead cats, dead rats, dead dogs, all of which are buried in the ground. You would think that after thousands and millions of years the earth beneath us would be filled with germs of death and disease! But in the intervention of God, He put something down in that ground. We have just recently discovered it. It is called penicillin. When you bury dead rats and dead cats and any dead thing, penicillin immediately destroys all of the disease in order that we might have a beautiful and healthful world upon which to walk and to live. Praise to God!

Consider the world within us—inside us. There is a law of psychology and sociology that says that out of the slums, ghettos, and vile environment come the flotsam and jetsam of human life—the sleazy, unkempt, dirty, and evil characters that scare us to death. It is that kind of a breeding ground that creates characters like that. So says the law of psychology and sociology.

Many years ago in West Dallas, which at that time was a breeding ground for the most unthinkable of characters, lived the Hamilton family with two boys, one named Floyd and the other named Raymond. In that same area of the city lived Clyde Barrow and Bonnie Parker. Raymond Hamilton was executed in the electric chair in Huntsville penitentiary. Clyde Barrow was shot down in an ambush, and his girl friend, Bonnie Parker, was slain with him. But Floyd Hamilton was sent to Alcatraz in San Francisco Bay.

In our dear First Baptist Church membership was a member named Hattie Rankin Moore, whom I had baptized. She, loving those dear people in West Dallas, came to me and said, "Would you go out to Alcatraz to see Floyd Hamilton?" I said that I would go and I did. Behind countless steel walls and doors and iron bars, I met with Floyd Hamilton. In the middle of the Alcatraz Prison, I extended my hand to him and asked, "If you will give your life to God, would you take my hand?" He warmly grasped my hand and said, "If God ever lets me live to get out of this prison, the first thing I will do is walk down that aisle in your church, confess my faith in Jesus, and be baptized." After many years, when he was finally freed, he came down the aisle, committing his life to God. I baptized him, and from that day forward he went all over the world telling people what great things God had done for him. That is the Lord at work! That is the miracle of God's intervention!

It is the same way with the world beyond and above us. The law of history says that nations rise to affluence, become corrupt, and finally fall back into slavery and death—a pattern that has littered nations along the shores of history. That is the law of history. All nations rise and fall. I never saw a Hittite; I never saw a Jebusite; I never saw a Moabite. But God told Ezekiel to look at the valley of dry bones. He told him he would cause breath to enter into them and they would live. And He breathed over that valley of very dry bones and there arose a great army for God (Ezek. 37). And the Lord told Jeremiah His prophet that as long as there was a sun to shine in the sky, and as long as there was a moon to shine by night, just so long would Israel as a people live before him (Jer. 31:35–37). It is all God.

It is the law of organizations that they flourish for a moment and then you never hear of them again. There are uncounted thousands of organizations that have resolved and dissolved before our eyes—except one. Jesus said, ". . . upon this rock I will build my church; and the gates of hell shall not prevail against it" (Matt. 16:18). In the Book of Revelation John writes of the consummation of the age:

> And there came unto me one of the seven angels which had the seven vials full of the seven last plagues, and talked with me, saying, Come hither, I will show thee the bride, the Lamb's wife [the church].
>
> And he carried me away in the spirit to a great and high mountain, and showed me that great city, the holy Jerusalem, descending out of heaven from God.
>
> Having the glory of God: and her light was like unto a stone most precious, even like a jasper stone, clear as crystal;
>
> And the building of the wall of it was of jasper: and the city was pure gold, like unto clear glass.
>
> And he showed me a pure river of water of life, clear as crystal, proceeding out of the throne of God and of the Lamb.
>
> In the midst of the street of it, and on either side of the river, was there the tree of life, which bare twelve manner of fruits, and yielded her fruit every month: and the leaves of the tree were for the healing of the nations.
>
> And there shall be no more curse: but the throne of God and of the Lamb shall be in it; and his servants shall serve him:
>
> And there shall be no night there; and they need no candle, neither light of the sun; for the Lord God giveth them light: and they shall reign for ever and ever (Rev. 21:9–11, 18; 22:1–3, 5).

As God put His sun to shine in the sky, as God revealed His Son to speak to us out of the Holy Scriptures, so He gave both to us for the light of the world and the salvation of our souls. The first great, omnipotent, universal fact is the reality of God!

3

What Is Wrong With Being an Atheist?

The fool hath said in his heart, There is no God. . . . (Ps. 14:1).

One of the strangest phenomenon that you could ever discover is that in the Bible from beginning to ending there is never any argument, defense, presentation, or forensic discussion concerning the existence, the reality, and the being of God. God is just presented and that is all.

"In the beginning . . . God" the Old Covenant unfolds. The New Covenant begins in the same way, "In the beginning was the *Logos*," the "reason," the "activity," the "manifestation" of God, by whom all things were created.

And the Word [*logos*] was made flesh, and dwelt among us, (and we beheld his glory, the glory as of the only begotten of the Father,) full of grace and truth. . . . For the law was given by Moses, but grace and truth came by Jesus Christ (John 1:14, 17).

There is never any defense, never any argument—just the avowal and presentation of the might, wonder, glory, and presence of God. The only exception to that is the brief, almost contemptuous, constigation and characterization of the fool who says in his heart, "There is no God."

The presentation of God in the Bible just says, "Here He is, look at Him." You have an instance like that when a man introduces the President of the United States. The more insignificant and lilliputian a man is, the more necessary is a laborious introduction. But when you present the President of the United

States, it is always this, "Ladies and Gentlemen, the President of the United States!" That is the way the Bible presents God. No argument for His existence, no defense of His reality, no long, endless elaboration of whether He is or not, just "This is God."

In my mind I have tried to understand why the Bible does not have an elaboration upon the existence of God or any argument for His being, or any extensive apologies defending the reality of God. There is just this observation, "The fool says that He does not exist."

There are four reasons why I think God said, "The fool hath said in his heart, There is no God." (1) The questions of the atheist are inane and irrelevant. (2) The speculative, defensive words of the atheist are empty and sterile. (3) The atheist is bankrupt in character. Character, morality, and righteousness are always grounded in almighty God. Wrong is wrong and right is right forever because God says it is so. (4) The death of the atheist is always ignoble.

HIS QUESTIONS ARE INANE AND IRRELEVANT

In the ancient Athenian world there lived a glorious thinker and philosopher by the name of Plato. He taught in the Academy. There Plato gathered his students. I can see Plato as he stood before those students, surrounded by his great masterpieces, the scrolls he had written, those Socratic dialogues, including that incomparable piece of literature, *The Republic.*

Or I think of Aristotle standing in the Lyceum, his school, with pupils before him. I see him surrounded by the masterpieces he has written, the scrolls on physics—what a man can touch, and metaphysics—that which is intangible and beyond what a man can touch.

I see Zeno standing on the stoa, speaking to his pupils, who were called "Stoics." He is surrounded by the masterpieces of literature.

As Plato stands in the midst of his masterpieces, a student in the Academy stands up and says, "Do you exist?" Or as Aristotle stands in the midst of the Lyceum, one of his students stands up and says, "Do you exist?" Or as Zeno teaches on the stoa, one of his Stoics looks at Zeno and asks, "Do you exist?" Only the fool would ask such a question.

Raphael must have been a handsome man. His face, his

countenance, his figure were amazingly comely. His spirit was gentle and kind. Everyone loved and admired Raphael. He was one of the most gifted painters of all time. He built his home next to St. Peter's, and there he had fifty students. I can imagine Raphael standing in the midst of those tremendous masterpieces he had painted, *The Coronation of the Virgin, The Sistine Madonna, The Transfiguration.* I can think of one of his pupils standing up and looking at Raphael in the midst of those tremendous masterpieces and asking, "Do you exist?"

Thomas Alva Edison, the incomparable inventor, stands in the midst of his inventions in the vast laboratory built for him in West Orange, New Jersey. He stands there before the electric light, the battery, the phonograph, and a thousand other things that bless our daily lives, and one of his pupils stands up and asks, "Edison, do you exist?"

The fool has said in his heart, "God, You do not exist!" Yet the Lord stands before us talking, walking, living, speaking, commanding, abjuring, pleading, blessing. He stands in the midst of His great masterpieces. The very heavens declare the glory of God! Day unto day the whole earth shows His marvelous handiwork. The fool asks, "Do you exist?" What is wrong with being an atheist? The questions of an atheist are irrelevant, impertinent, and sometimes silly and insulting.

Francis Bacon, the great essayist of England, wrote this little sentence: "A little philosophy inclineth man's mind to atheism, but depth in philosophy bringeth men's minds about to religion."

Listen to this shrewd observation written by John Foster (1770-1843) about an atheist:

> The wonder turns on the great process by which a man could grow to the immense intelligence that can know there is no God. This intelligence involves the very attributes of Deity. For unless the man is omnipresent, in some place where he is not, there may be God. If he does not know absolutely every agent in the universe, the one that he does not know may be God. If he is not himself the chief agent in the universe and does not know what is so, that which is so may be God. If he is not in absolute possession of all the propositions that constitute universal truth, the one which he lacks may be that there is a God. If he cannot with certainty assign the cause of all that he perceives to exist, that cause may be a God. If he does not know everything that has been done in immeasurable ages past, some things may have been done by a God. Thus, unless he knows all things, that is, precludes another Deity by being one himself, he

cannot know that the Being whose existence he rejects does not
exist.

That man was smart! Let me illustrate that another way, which
may not be as smart, but it surely does avow the same thing!

A skeptic came up to a little boy and said, "Son, I will give
you this big red apple if you will tell me where God is." The little
boy immediately replied, "Mister, I'll give you a whole barrel of
'em if you will show me where He ain't!"

Why does God say, "The fool hath said in his heart, There is
no God" and then dismiss it? The first answer that came to my
heart was that the questions of the fool are irrelevant and inane.
The second answer concerns the discussions of the atheist.

His Speculations Are Empty and Sterile

The discussions, the diatribes, the affirmations, the forensics
of the atheist are empty and sterile, vapid and void.

A tremendous, recurring, and resounding note in the Bible is
found in Psalm 111:10, in Proverbs 1:7, and in Proverbs 9:10.
You know it well. "The fear of the LORD is the beginning of wis-
dom." The beginning of wisdom is the reverential awe of God.
The beginning of wisdom is bowing before the great, omnipotent
Creator.

A senior in college said to a freshman who had just enrolled,
"What would you think if in ten minutes I gave you arguments
that would simply annihilate God?" The freshman replied, "Sir, I
would think the same thing as if a gnat were to climb up the side
of Pike's Peak and say, 'Watch me pulverize this mountain with
my left hind foot in ten minutes!' " The arguments of the atheists
are sterile and void.

A hoptoad and a green lizard in West Texas were watching
an express train go hurtling by. The hoptoad said: "You know,
they tell me that somebody made that train. What idiocy! It made
itself." Then the green lizard said: "You know, they tell me that
there is an engineer that drives that train. What inanity! It drives
itself." A red ant overheard their talking, climbed up on the top of
a spike, and said, "They tell me there is a president of this rail-
road system. If there is, I defy him to come here and strike me
dead!" God said, "The fool! Why should I take time to strike him
dead!"

The atheists present remarkable arguments. They never give

an intelligent answer to the great mystery of the cosmos around us. They, or humanists as we call them today, never give an intelligent answer to the meaning of a man's life and work in this earth. On the other hand, it is a remarkable thing that with the eyes of the soul we penetrate into the deep, everlasting truth and mysteries of God and His creation.

The apostle Paul wrote of that in Romans 1:19–20:

> That which may be known of God is manifest in them; for God hath showed it unto them.
> For the invisible things of him from the creation of the world are clearly seen, being understood by the things that are made, even his eternal power and Godhead. . . .

Is this a contradiction in words—"The invisible things . . . are clearly seen"? The apostle says the invisible things from God are clearly seen, being understood by the things that are, even the eternal power of the godhead. When you look at that contradiction in terms, then you begin to understand the great truth of the world around you, for there are invisible and unseen laws and powers that govern gravity, motion, physics, chemistry, dynamics, thermodynamics, biology, and on and on we could go. Over and beyond what our physical eyes can see are great invisible truths that guide and mold and control our universe and our being. The man who is able to see with the eyes of his soul, with the eyes of faith, finds the secret of the universe in matter, in mind, in soul, in heart, or in life, and it leads him to God.

The answers, the discussions, the metaphysics of the atheists are empty and sterile. It is like drinking at a mirage that never quenches thirst. It is like eating ephemeral food that never satisfies hunger. It is like reading a book that has no meaning. It is like building a house without a plan. It is like riding a train without an engineer. It is like living a life without purpose and without meaning. God says it is a fool who says there is no God.

HIS CHARACTER IS BANKRUPT

When I think of that characterization, "The fool hath said in his heart, There is no God, I cannot help but think that not only are his questions irrelevant, not only are his discussions vapid and void, but also his character is bankrupt. When I studied the Bible preparing this chapter, I realized for the first time that when Paul was presenting the truth of the depravity of humanity in Romans 3, he quoted this psalm. All humanity has fallen, our minds are fallen, our wills are fallen, our desires are fallen, our lives are fallen. We belong to a fallen race. What God is apparently saying to us, as the apostle Paul expounds it, is this: When a man denies God he floods the earth with evil and wickedness. That is universally true. The incontrovertible, unalterable, and irrefutable truth inevitably follows that when a people deny God, wickedness and wrong flood the land. Character and God go together. When a man leaves God out of his life and denies the existence of God, character rots.

A Dallas television and radio station invited me to debate Madalyn Murray O'Hair, the famous feminist atheist in America. The people in my church said, "Pastor, do not do that." In one of those aberrations of pastoral response, I did it anyway. We were to debate for four hours. They seated us before reporters from all over the nation. The man who was emceeing the event said, "Now, you reporters may ask them any question you desire." A young reporter from the *Houston Chronicle* jumped up first. He asked a question that lit Mrs. O'Hair's fuse and set fire to her shuck! It hammered on her detonation cap! She blew up! She turned vitriolic and livid! Do you know what the question was? That young fellow looked at me and asked, "Dr. Criswell, do you feel that you have stooped in condescension to debate that atheist sitting by you?" She hit the ceiling! That made her furious! Well, I was going to answer nicely, but I never got a word in. She just blew up! When we started into the actual debate, she was absolutely livid.

Because of the arrangement of the studio, and the guests that were there, we had to sit very close together. I was sitting about three or four inches from her. During the four hours, there were commericals every fifteen minutes. She talked to me throughout them all. I cannot quote what that atheist said to me. It was a new experience for me!

Then some years later I read in the *Dallas Morning News*:

> William Murray, son of Madalyn Murray O'Hair, says miracles have happened in his life since he denounced atheism and gave his life to God.
> Sixteen-year-old Murray was the plaintiff in his mother's 3-year court battle that began in 1963 and resulted in the U.S. Supreme Court decision to ban state-mandated prayer in public schools.

He stunned the Christian community last month when he said he was born again into Christianity and made a public apology for his role in his mother's suit.

"I began searching for meaning in my life, thinking surely there has to be something else than this. My self-search for communion and meaning brought me to my knees, and since then there have been miracles in my life. The alcohol vanished. Four packs of cigarettes a day vanished.

"The minister told me perhaps I needed to make some amends, so I decided when I got back to Texas to apologize to the segments of society I had injured by my participation in the 1963 court decision on prayer.

"Having done that, I felt a relaxation of the burden I had carried through that involvement. My life has changed."

I have a long article from a national magazine regarding his marvelous conversion.

The bankruptcy of character that inevitably follows atheism is abundantly evident in the lifestyle of Madalyn Murray O'Hair. For example, here is a statement from her published in a national magazine.

I'd describe myself as a sexual libertarian. I will engage in sexual activity with any consenting male any time I damn well please. Sex is where you find it.

I have had five affairs, all of them real wing-dings. I have enjoyed every damn minute of them.

I think young people should be able to have their first sexual love affair whenever they feel like it. In the case of most girls, this would be around 13 or 14; with most boys, around 15 or 16.

Whenever they want to try it, they should be allowed to go at it without supervision or restriction—in their parents' bedroom, on the grass in a park, in a motel; it doesn't matter.

That is atheism! "The fool hath said in his heart, There is no God."

His Ultimate Decease Is Ignoble

But there is a fourth reason why the Bible calls the atheist a fool. His ultimate decease is ignoble.

In 1899, in London, England, a Society for the Advancement of Atheism was organized. A few years ago, at one of their annual banquets, the president of the Society stood up and made a toast in which he referred to the apostle Paul: "To the apostle Paul who was blinded on the road to Damascus and who has stayed blind ever since!" The audience laughed and applauded until the president who made the toast was seen to totter and to fall. When they went to his assistance, he was dead. The banquet fell into confusion and dismay.

My predecessor in the First Baptist Church in Muskogee, Oklahoma, was called "the George W. Truett of Oklahoma." He looked and spoke like Dr. Truett. He was a great, mighty man of God, and he was pastor of the church in Muskogee twenty-eight years. He said to his deacons, "When I lay down this mantle, I want you to call Dr. Criswell as my successor." Christmas Eve, 1940, he closed his eyes on this world and opened them in heaven. When they approached his desk, the sermon he was preparing at the time of his death was entitled, "My First Five Minutes in Heaven." On the first Sunday in January, they appointed a pulpit committee at 12:30 in the afternoon, and at 1:00 they called me as pastor. For God's servants death is triumphant; it is the beginning and not the ending.

More than forty years ago in South Carolina, I listened for the first time to the most eloquent preacher Southern Baptists ever produced, Robert G. Lee. In his message he spoke about his dear, sainted mother. He said that as a boy he had gone with his mother to visit an old black "mammy." Today we would call her a household servant. She was a saint of God. He said that as his mother sat by the bed of that dying woman, the servant turned to her and said, "Mrs. Lee, I is a gettin' ready to trade this ol' wore out wagon for a golden chariot."

> A lookin' over Jordan, and what did I see?
> Comin' for to carry me home.
> A band of angels a comin' after me,
> Comin' for to carry me home.
>
> Swing low, sweet chariot,
> Comin' for to carry me home.
> Swing low, sweet chariot,
> Comin' for to carry me home.

God says that a man is a fool who denies the Lord and rejects the faith. And that means that the man is blessed who gives his heart to God, who loves the Lord, who rears his children in the love and nurture of Christ Jesus. Oh, what a God-blessed open door the Lord has set before us!

4

He That Cometh to God

> . . . for he that cometh to God must believe that he is, and that he is a rewarder of them that diligently seek him (Heb. 11:6b).

The eleventh chapter of Hebrews is one of the great chapters in the Word of God, one of the high mountain peaks of the Bible. It is a roll call of the heroes of the faith.

It could be given the title "Seeing the Invisible" or "Seeing With the Eyes of Faith." That is how we see God. In the third verse, the writer declares that "things which are seen were not made of things which do appear." The things that we see are made of things that we cannot see. In Greek, this is the finest statement of the atomic, molecular constitution and structure of matter that you will find in any human speech.

In verse 7 we read, "Noah, being warned of God of things not seen as yet," believed God. In verse 10, Abraham, Isaac, and Jacob were looking "for a city which hath foundations, whose builder and maker is God." And the answer in verse 16 is triumphant, "Wherefore God is not ashamed to be called their God: for he hath prepared for them a city."

In verse 19 Abraham, in offering up Isaac, believed God would raise Isaac from the dead. Verse 27 is one of the finest descriptive verses in the Bible. Moses chose rather to suffer affliction with the people of God than to enjoy the pleasures of sin for a season. "By faith [Moses] forsook Egypt, not fearing the wrath of the king: for he endured, as seeing him who is invisible."

He That Cometh to God

THE CONCEPT OF FAITH

Faith is one of the greatest words in any language. By faith the farmer plows the soil and sows his seed, believing and trusting God for a harvest. By faith the doctor opens the body, performs a surgical operation, believing and trusting God for the healing. By faith the banker opens his doors and invites the depositers to come in and trust him with their possessions. Business and life are impossible without faith.

Did you ever notice how the business world cannot escape using the language of faith, the language of the church? A woman called the bank about her bonds. The banker asked her: "What denomination are your securities? Are you interested in conversion or redemption?" There was a long pause on the telephone line and the woman finally asked, "Am I talking to the First National Bank or the First Baptist Church?" You cannot escape it. All of life is put together in those words. By faith, lovers build a home and rear their children. Faith plows the soil, sails the sea, builds our institutions. By faith we see God.

THE EYES OF THE SOUL

There is a faculty that God has given to man, an inward sight, the eyes of the soul. With those eyes, seeing the invisible, we come to know God. That is the faculty that distinguishes a man from the rest of God's creation. Man is able to see the unseen. All of the marvels of our twentieth-century modern life are the results of man's seeing the invisible. Radio, radar, television, nylon, jet propulsion, atomic fission, penicillin—all of the wonders that come to us in this new world in which we live have been here from the beginning of the creation. It is just now with eyes of faith that we are beginning to see the invisible things and to pluck them out of the unknown. So it is with God. We see Him with the eyes of our soul everywhere—above us, around us, beneath us, and inside of us.

An agnostic, a skeptic, an infidel, an atheist replies, "But I do not see Him." Neither does the clod in the fresh broken furrow, neither does the beast in the field. A dog in his kennel is utterly oblivious to the glorious firmament above him. The cow grazing in the pasture is not sensitive to the glorious landscape all around her. To the spiritually blind, the light of God does not shine. To the spiritually deaf, the revelation of God never speaks. To the spiritually dead, the life of God never exists. To many the stars are just planets up there in the heavens, but to a psalmist they proclaim the glory of God. To many, a tree is just root and trunk and leaves, but to a Joyce Kilmer:

> I think that I will never see
> A poem lovely as a tree.
> A tree whose hungry mouth is pressed
> Against the earth's sweet loving breast;
> A tree that looks at God all day,
> And lifts her leafy arms to pray;
>
> Poems are made by fools like me,
> But only God could make a tree.

Alfred Lord Tennyson could see the very essence of God in the smallest, most inconsequential flower.

> Flower, in the crannied wall,
> I pluck you out of the crannies,
> I hold you here, root and all, in my hand,
> Little flower—but if I could understand
> What you are, root and all, and all in all,
> I could know what God and man is.

The eyes of faith see God everywhere—they see the invisible. William Herbert Carruth wrote so eloquently when he said:

> A haze on the far horizon,
> The infinite tender sky,
> The rich ripe tint of the cornfields,
> And the wild geese sailing by;
> And all over upland and lowland
> The charm of the goldenrod,
> Some of us call it autumn,
> And others call it God.

The skeptic says, "That is not enough. I want to see Him. I want Him to stand here before me and announce, 'I am God.' I want to look at Him standing in my presence." Those are words of the egotistical, self-exalting man. It is a strange thing how imperious of heart man can be.

In 63 B.C., Pompey conquered Judea and added it as a province to the Roman empire. He came marching into Jerusalem with his conquering legions and made his way up to the temple area and into the sanctuary. He put his hand on the veil to draw aside the Holy of Holies. When the Jewish people saw what he was doing, they bowed down before him and asked that he take their lives rather than desecrate the Holy of Holies, into which the high priest entered beyond the veil once a year with blood for atonement. Proud, arrogant Pompey with imperious disdain pulled aside the veil, and for the first time a pagan entered into the Holy of Holies. He walked around. Then he came back out and made the exclamation: "Why, there is nothing in it! It is empty!" Yet that is the place where Isaiah said:

> I saw also the Lord . . . high and lifted up, and his train filled the temple.
> Above it stood the seraphim:. . . .
> And one cried unto another, and said, Holy, holy, holy, is the Lord of hosts: the whole earth is full of his glory (Is. 6:1–3).

Pompey had visions of personal grandeur when he entered the Holy of Holies to seize the God of the Hebrews. "I will take this God of the Hebrews and I will put him on a wagon, and he will grace my triumph as I ride through the streets of Rome, the conquerer of Judea and Jehovah!" That is man for you! He wants God to be used, to be displayed! He wants Him here before us to look at Him!

But it may be that it is not only an infidel or an imperious pagan like Pompey who seeks to use God. When we read the Bible, we are almost astonished that those saints of the Old Testament cry, just as some of us do, "Lord, where are You!" Job asked, "Wherefore hidest thou they face, and holdest me for thine enemy?" (13:24). Again in Job 23:3, he said, "Oh that I knew where I might find him! That I might come even to his seat!" David cried pathetically in Psalm 10:1, "Why standest thou afar off, O Lord? why hidest thou thyself in times of trouble?" Again in Psalm 13:1 he says, "How long wilt thou forget me, O Lord? for ever? how long wilt thou hide thy face from me?" Isaiah cried in Isaiah 45:15, "Verily thou art a God that hidest thyself, O God of Israel, the Savior." And again the prophet prays in Isaiah 64:1–2, "Oh that thou wouldest rend the heavens, that thou wouldest come down, that the mountains might flow down at they presence, as when the melting fire burneth, the fire causeth the waters to boil, to make thy name known to thine adversaries, that the nations may tremble at thy presence!" In John 14, after Philip had been with the Lord for three years, he said, "Lord, show us the Father, and it sufficeth us."

Does God stand before some proscenium and say, "Look, here is God"? Or does He come down in some vast demonstration, perhaps in the Cotton Bowl or at some important inauguration, and say, "Look, here is God"? There are three things that God says and does in answer to the appeal that He show Himself for our personal touch.

GOD COVERS HIMSELF IN CREATION

God clothes Himself in Creation. No man can see God and live. John wrote about it, "No man hath seen God at any time" (1:18). Our minds are not able to contain infinitude. Our brains would burst! Our senses cannot receive the omnipotence of the Almighty. Our sinful natures cannot bear the presence of the holiness of God. Why, we cannot even look at the sun! The only way I can look at the sun is to shade my eyes with heavy glasses. How then could I expect to look upon the face of God!

In Exodus 33, Moses asked, "God, let me see You." And God answered:

> Thou canst not see my face: for there shall no man see me, and live.
> And the LORD said, Behold, there is a place by me, and thou shalt stand upon a rock:
> And it shall come to pass, while my glory passeth by, that I will put thee in a clift of the rock, and will cover thee with my hand while I pass by:
> And I will take away mine hand, and thou shalt see my back parts: but my face shall not be seen (Ex. 33:20–23).

God shut up Moses in that cleft of the rock and covered him with His hand. And when the glory of God passed by, the Lord took away His hand and Moses saw the afterglow of the garments of the *shekinah* glory of the Almighty. We cannot see God and live.

God clothes Himself in the marvelous creation around us. A man is terrified and devastated at the mere appearance of an angel. Anytime an angel appears, it is with the assuring words, "Fear not" or "Do not be afraid." How much more if God were to appear! With one hand He fashions a golden ring six hundred and seventy thousand miles in diameter to swing around Saturn, and with the other hand He fashions the point of the claw on the foot of a microscopic insect. That is God! One day placing in the universe a blazing sun ninety-three million miles away, and the next day painting the face of a little flower with the colors of His rainbow, and dropping in its chaliced heart a little bit of perfume in order that it might attract an insect to fertilize an ovule. That is God! His hands of master workmanship are everywhere! He clothes Himself in this marvelous universe!

In the city of Rome in the latter days of Michelangelo, when the great artist was blind, they discovered statuary buried in the heaps. "It must be Grecian," they said. They sent for Michelangelo. Michelangelo, in his blindness and with his sensitive hands, felt of the statue—the eyebrow, the forehead, the nose, the contour of the face, the shoulders. Blind Michelangelo said: "It is the work of a great master. It must have been made by Phidias." That is the way with us. We follow the contours of God's incomparable and marvelous creation. It must have been made by a master workman. It looks like the hands of God. God clothes Himself, He hides Himself, God presents Himself in His glorious creation.

God Covers Himself in Human Flesh

God presents Himself, He clothes Himself with human flesh. The most marvelous of all the miracles of the Lord God is that He became man. That is a truth beyond what my mind can understand. Thy mystery of godliness is that God was manifest in the flesh.

> In the beginning was the Word, and the Word was with God, And the Word was God.
> And the Word was made flesh, and dwelt among us, (and we beheld his glory, the glory as of the only begotten of the Father,) full of grace and truth (John 1:1, 14).

God was veiled in human flesh.

Sometimes the deity of our Lord shone through the veil of His flesh. On Mt. Hermon He was transfigured before His three closest disciples, and His countenance was as the sun shining in its strength and His raiment became as white as snow. The deity of God shone through the veil of His flesh.

When He was asleep in the boat, the disciples awakened Him in the midst of the storm and cried, "Master, carest thou not that we perish?" Then the record continues, "And he arose, and rebuked the wind, and said unto the sea, Peace, be still" (Mark

4:38b–39a). The deity of God was shining through the veil of His flesh.

When the soldiers arrested Him, they said, "We seek Jesus of Nazareth." Jesus said unto them, "I am he. . . ." Then what happened? "As soon then as he had said unto them, I am he, they went backward, and fell to the ground" (John 18:6). The deity of the Lord shone through the veil of His flesh.

The Book of Hebrews says that through that parted, torn veil He entered into glory and made a way for us to follow after. Oh, the wonder of God's marvelous revelation of Himself when He clothed Himself with human flesh!

GOD COVERS HIMSELF IN HUMAN EXPERIENCE

God clothes Himself in the providences and the experiences of life. We see Him, the invisible, sometimes in the tragedies of sorrows and tears of our lives.

There was a businessman who had no time for God or the church. He was too busy for such trifles and extraneous invitations as that. His little boy went to a Sunday school. One day a little fellow knocked at the man's door. The big businessman came to the door and the little boy excitedly said, "Your boy was on his bicycle down the street and a car hit him!" The father rushed down the street. There he saw the little boy's bicycle all crushed and twisted and covered with blood. He asked the little group of lads gathered around, "Where is my boy?" They answered: "We do not know. The car that hit him took him away."

The man rushed to his home and began to call all the hospitals in the city. "Do you have a little boy badly hurt who has just been admitted?" Finally one of the hospitals answered, "Yes, he is here." The father made his way to the hospital. There lay his little boy crushed and broken. As he sat by the side of the lad, he took his hand.

The little boy said, "Daddy, pray." The father said, "Son, I do not pray." The little boy said, "Please Daddy, pray." The father answered, "Son, I do not know how to pray!" The little lad said, "Daddy, in Sunday school I learned to pray a prayer. Would you pray it with me?" The lad started, "Our Father who art in heaven." The father repeated, "Our Father who art in heaven." "Hallowed be thy name." The daddy repeated, "Hallowed be thy name." The little boy prayed, "Thy kingdom come." The father continued, "Thy kingdom come." Then the little boy added, "Thy will be done." The father refused. "Thy will be done." The father refused. The little boy said, "Daddy, pray it, pray it, 'Thy will be done.' " While the father continued to refuse, the hand of the little boy went limp. The father looked into the boy's face and he was gone! The father fell down on the floor, and in an agony of hurt and a flood of tears, he prayed that prayer, "Thy will be done!" Instantaneously, God came into his soul, and he was marvelously and wonderfully converted.

Well, you say, that is abnormal. Does such a thing as that really happen? I close with a word from one of the greatest intellects America has ever produced. Dr. Charles Hodge, who for over fifty years in this last century was head of the department of theology at Princeton University, wrote one of the greatest volumes on systematic theology ever penned by man. From that I quote:

> Whatever arouses the moral nature, whether it be danger, or suffering, or the approach of death, banishes unbelief in a moment. Men pass from skepticism to faith instantaneously, not by a process of argument, but by the existence of a state of consciousness with which skepticism is irreconcilable and in the process of which unbelief cannot exist.

Maybe we are self-sufficient in times of our strength in manhood and womanhood. But in the hour of being crushed or hurt or dissolved in tears, instantly, without argument, we come to see God. It is a wonderful discovery—seeing God all around us and in us, seeing God in the face of Jesus Christ, the veil of His deity, and finding God in the providences of life.

Lord, in Thy presence I bow in humble faith and in quiet acceptance. In Thy blessing, dear God, let me live, let me die, and let me hope for a more glorious and triumphant tomorrow!

5

Is There a God Who Cares About Me?

Does God really care about me? Does He know my name? Does He know that I exist? Does He know anything about me? Is there a God who watches over me?

> As the hart panteth after the water brooks, so panteth my soul after thee, O God.
> My soul thirsteth for God, for the living God: when shall I come and appear before God?
> My tears have been my meat day and night, while they continually say unto me, Where is thy God? (Ps. 42:1–3).

It often seems that all of the things that we know and see in life disprove any interest of a higher omnipotence in us and in our welfare. As one scientist said: "We are alone in the universe. We are orphans." Another scientist said, "The silence of infinitude terrifies me." Is there anyone in my life and in a life to come who has any regard for me?

Practically everything that we know argues for our inconsequential insignificance. The astronomers in describing the vast infinitude of creation refer to our whole world as a small speck in the great and vast spectrum of God's creation. On this earth the mountains seemingly raise their heads in helplessness. The deep valleys are depressions of hopelessness. The very oceans are reservoirs of blood, murder, violence, and war. The rivers of the earth are streams of tears springing forth from the brokenheartedness of humanity. In our own lives and on the planet in which we live, we seem to be like autumnal leaves falling by the immeasurable, uncounted millions to the ground, there to perish with all the other leaves that fall. This earth is nothing other than one vast, illimitable cemetery in which we bury our dead.

In my reading, I discovered a magazine picture of a vast ocean moved by some terrific wind. Above the picture was the caption "Who Cares For Me," and beneath was this caption: "Nobody cares about me. I feel like a tiny, insignificant speck trapped in the turbulence of humanity, tossed back and forth by forces beyond my control."

In one of my pastorates, a funeral director asked me to conduct the service of a man unknown to me. When I went to the funeral home, there was nobody with the deceased. The funeral director asked, "Would you get at least one person to be a witness so that if I am ever questioned, I could prove that the man had a decent Christian burial?" I went out on the streets. I found a hamburger shop, and I asked the owner if he would come and be with me in the service. I conducted the service with that one man there sharing the hour. What was the name of that man I buried? Does God know him? Was it any matter to the Lord? Where is his grave? Can God distinguish the dust of that fallen humanity from the rest of the dust of the ground? Is there a God who cares about me? Does He know me? Does He know my name?

A postgraduate student went to Nikko, a Japanese city of shrines to many gods. Failing to find God among the shrines, he went to a great waterfall in the mountains and wrote this note:

> I have gone through the difficult task of education seeking for God, but I have failed. I came to Nikko and continued that search to find God and there I failed. I am now going into the other world to see if I can find God there.

The article said that he leaped into the mad, swirling rapids and plunged over the precipice to his death. In a few succeeding years, 286 students followed him, until the government was forced to take measures to prevent the awful succession of suicides.

Where is God? Where do I find God? Is there a God who cares about me? Finally and ultimately all of us come to that deep, indescribable longing and hungering and yearning. Where is God? Youth and beauty soon fade away. The suicide of Marilyn Monroe is attributed to the fact that as the days went by, she saw her beauty was departing. Rather than face the inevitable, she took her own life.

There is in Dallas a wealthy man of tremendous executive ability and success. But he is getting older. His money cannot buy health and length of days. As he is facing an ultimate darkness, he is beginning to ask, "Where is God?" Finally, all of us are brought to that yearning hunger, "Is there a God who cares about me? I want God."

A father stood by the open grave. There were three little children clutching at his garments, unaware of what was happening. That father watched his wife lowered into the grave below. When he and his children went home, the three children went through the house crying, "Mommy, where are you?" The father gathered the children to him and said, "I will be your mother?" The children burst out, "We want Mommy!" When time came to put them to bed, he went next door to a sweet, neighborly mother and asked her to come and put the children to bed. She hugged them and kissed them and tucked them in and said, "I will be your mother." But all three cried, "We want Mommy!" They cried themselves to sleep wanting Mommy. We are children just like that. When youth is gone, when life is gone, when money can buy nothing else, and when we face an ultimate and inevitable tomorrow, who is out there? Does He know me? Is He my friend? Does He care about me? That cry for God is in our deepest soul.

What is your soul? You cannot define it. You cannot look at it. You cannot see it. But whatever the soul is, it has within it that yearning and seeking after God. Where can I find God? In these stories of the human race, some have looked at the sun and said, "Are you God?" They have worshiped the sun. Some have looked at the moon and said, "Are you God?" They have worshiped the moon. Some have looked at the stars and said, "Are you God?" They have worshiped the stars. Some scientifically-minded people have looked at these unseen laws that govern all creation, and they have asked, "Are you God, a first primal cause?" Others have looked at mythological characters, and they have worshiped them on Mount Jupiter. Others in history have sought some incarnation in a Buddha, in a Zoroaster, or in a Krishna. Our souls ask, "Where is God?"

In my own heart, my own inner life, my deepest spirit, I am

50

conscious of Him. Where does He come from? How is it that He speaks to me in my deepest self? I ask my ear, "Did God come in through you?" My ear says, "All I can do is just hear sound." I ask my eye, "Did God come in through you?" My eye replies, "All I can see is light and color and lines." I ask my fingers, "Did God brush by you?" My fingers reply, "All I can do is sense tangible reality." Then how did God get into my heart? How is it that He moves in my spirit? How is it that He makes me want to find Him? It must be that there is a God who cares about me. It must be that God reaches down and touches me in my inmost soul, that He knocks at the door of my heart seeking my love, adoration, worship, and commitment of life. There must be a God who cares about me?

God Has a Personal Name Expressing His Care for Us

In the marvelous self-revelation of the Lord to us, our Lord has revealed Himself in a personal name that describes His loving, tender, and merciful care. God is somebody. He is not an "it." God is not the pervasive, impersonal, cosmic force of the earth. God is not the unseen laws that govern the universe. God is somebody. He is a person. He lives. He is not a law; He is life. The effort to depersonalize God would take away from Him any thought of His being understanding, sympathetic, loving, or forgiving. When we depersonalize God, we take away the rose and leave the thorn. When we depersonalize God, we take the sun out of the sky and leave nothing but abysmal midnight darkness. God is somebody, and He refers to Himself and to what is His thousands of times as "I" and "Me" and "Mine." He reveals Himself as a person. Did Enoch walk with cosmic law? Did Enoch walk with the great pervasive forces of the universe? No! Enoch walked with God!

Hagar, having been sent away from her home in Beersheba, wandered in the desert with her child Ishmael. There she put the child aside because she did not want to watch him die. The angel of God appeared and guided her to a fountain. God opened the eyes of Hagar to His loving provision (Gen. 21:9–20). God is somebody. God lives. God talks. God sees. He reveals Himself in a personal way. His very name signifies His care for us.

On the back side of the desert in a burning bush, the Lord God spoke to Moses and said: "Moses, I have seen the affliction

51

of my people, and I have heard their cry. Come now, and I will send you to deliver my people out of bondage." Moses said, "Lord, when I come before the people and tell them you have sent me and they ask me 'What is your Name, what shall I say?" The Lord God then told Moses His personal name (see Ex. 3). For thousands of years the Hebrew people were in such awe before the Lord God that they never spoke that name. Rather, they used some other term like "Adonai" or "El Shaddai," but never the personal name of God. Therefore, the pronunciation of His name has been lost. In the Bible we have taken the four consonants of the name of God and added to them the vowel pointings of the term "Adonai," meaning "Lord." That resulting word is "Jehovah." Maybe the best pronunciation of the Hebrew word, spoken as literally as we could ever know, would be *Yahweh*. God told Moses this: "You go tell them that my name is *Yahweh, Jehovah*, I AM THAT I AM." But the grammarians say to us that it would be a better translation to say: "Tell them my name is I WILL BE WHAT I WILL BE, Jehovah, *Yahweh*. When you go before the people in Israel and they ask you, 'What is My name?' You tell them that My name is 'I will be your deliverer, your guide, a pillar of fire by night and a pillar of cloud by day. You tell them I will be your shepherd.' "

Through the years Jehovah has loved and guided His people. I do not think there is anything more contrastingly meaningful in the entire Word of God than a verse that Isaiah places in the midst of the description of the infinitude of the Almighty:

> Behold, the nations are as a drop of a bucket, and are counted as the small dust of the balance: behold, he taketh up the isles as a very little thing.
> All nations before him are as nothing; and they are counted to him less than nothing, and vanity.
> To whom then will ye liken God? or what likeness will ye compare unto him? (Is. 40:15, 17, 18).

Then in the midst of that marvelous description of the omnipotence of the Almighty the prophet writes:

> He shall feed his flock like a shepherd: he shall gather the lambs with his arm, and carry them in his bosom, and shall gently lead those that are with young (Is. 40:11).

The great, mighty Creator of the world who faints not feeds His flock like a shepherd, gathers His lambs in His arms, carries them in His bosom, gently leads those that are with young. His name is I WILL BE YOUR DELIVERER, your Guide, your Savior, your Shepherd, your Companion through all of the years of your pilgrim way.

The whole revelation of God in the old covenant is just like that. Isaiah was sent by the Lord God back to Hezekiah, to whom he had just given the prophecy from the Lord that Hezekiah was to set his house in order because of his impending death. Hezekiah prayed and wept before the Lord, and God sent Isaiah back to the palace to announce to the king:

> I have heard thy prayer, I have seen thy tears: behold, I will add unto thy days fifteen years (Is. 38:5).

Such is God. His name is Jehovah. His name is *Yahweh.* His name means I WILL BE THAT I WILL BE. There is no end to His bounty. There is no end to His mercy and love. It expands with every generation and every age.

He Became One of Us—In Fashion As a Man

God says I will be your fellow pilgrim. I will be one of you. I will be made in fashion as a man. I will assume all of the vicissitudes and fortunes and providences of life. I will live and walk among you. That is My name. I will be your Savior, Companion, and Friend. I will live your life.

No wonder Paul proclaimed the great and holy mystery that God was manifest in the flesh, that God would be a man, that He would live a life like ours. The Gospel of Matthew begins with the narrative of God's incarnation.

> Then Joseph her husband, being a just man, and not willing to make her a public example, was minded to put her away privily.
>
> But while he thought on these things, behold, the angel of the Lord appeared unto him in a dream, saying, Joseph, thou son of David, fear not to take unto thee Mary thy wife: for that which is conceived in her is of the Holy Ghost.
>
> And she shall bring forth a son, and thou shalt call his name JESUS: for he shall save his people from their sins.
>
> Now all this was done, that it might be fulfilled which was spoken of the Lord by the prophet, saying,
>
> Behold, a virgin shall be with child, and shall bring forth a son, and they shall call his name Immanuel, which being interpreted is, God with us (Matt. 2:19–23).

God in human flesh is presented in the beautiful announcement of the angel Gabriel to Mary in Nazareth.

> And the angel answered and said unto her, The Holy Ghost shall come upon thee, and the power of the Highest shall overshadow thee: therefore also that holy thing which shall be born of thee shall be called the Son of God (Luke 1:35).

The great doctrinal treatises in the epistles are just like that. Jesus is God in human flesh.

> [Jesus] is the image of the invisible God, the firstborn of every creature (Col. 1:15).

> Who being the brightness of his glory, and the express image of his person, and upholding all things by the word of his power . . . (Heb. 1:3).

> Jesus saith unto him, Have I been so long time with you, and yet hast thou not known me, Philip? he that hath seen me hath seen the Father; and how sayest thou then, Show us the Father? (John 14:9).

This is God clothed in human flesh. What is God like? Does He care for me? What kind of a person is He?

In describing the Lord Jesus, the gospel writers say, "And when Jesus saw the multitudes, he was moved with compassion upon them." Jesus, moved with compassion, is His ever-endearing name. Jesus—how He loves us! He said that even the hairs on our heads are numbered. He not only knows our names, but He knows more about us than we know about ourselves. He told us that not one sparrow would fall to the ground without our Heavenly Father following its flight to the earth (Matt. 10:29). He taught us about the one lost sheep, the one lost coin, and then He added, "For the Son of man is come to seek and to save that which was lost" (Luke 19:10).

What is God like? What is Jesus like? Watch Him ministering—sensitively. Thronged on every side, He turned and said, "Someone touched Me." A woman with an issue of blood had said in her heart, "If I but touch the hem of His garment, I will be healed." Someone touched Me," He said. How sensitive He was!

Jesus is the channel through whom God cares for us and loves us. His preaching from village to village and from house to house ministering to the people, His healing their illnesses, His opening their eyes, His cleansing of the lepers, His preaching to the poor—all are beautiful examples of the ministering work of our wonderful Lord! Weeping at the tomb of Lazarus, crying over the lost city of Jerusalem, weeping for our sins in Gethsemane, dying for us, He endured those agonies of travail in spirit and soul into which we cannot enter because He became sin for us. This the God who cares did for us!

Finally, according to the author of the Book of Hebrews, He is in heaven "at the right hand of the Majesty on high." He is a faithful High Priest and compassionate intercessor who is moved and touched by the feeling of our infirmities. Nobody is poor but that He was poor. Nobody is hungry but that He was hungry. Nobody suffers but that He has suffered. Nobody is hurt but that He was hurt. Nobody cries but that He cried. Nobody is disappointed but that he was disappointed. Nobody is in agony but that He was in agony. Our great and merciful High Priest is moved with the feeling of our infirmities. "Wherefore," the Book of Hebrews says, "Come boldly unto the throne of grace, that [ye] may find . . . help in time of need" (Heb. 4:15–16). This is the great God who cares for us, *Yahweh,* Jehovah.

John says that when Isaiah saw the Lord Jehovah high and lifted up, he saw Jesus (John 12). Jehovah, *Yahweh,* is His name in the Old Covenant, the same God who is moved in His heart by our afflictions. "I have heard the cry of my people. I have seen their affliction." Jehovah of the Old Testament is the Lord Jesus of the New Testament, moved with compassion and touched with the feeling of our infirmities. There is no doubt but that sin has in it a judgment, but it is God who shows Himself toward us, not bitter, but always compassionate and merciful. He is a great, forgiving God. That is His name. *Yahweh*—I will be that I will be.

He Is With Us Forever

God promises that He will be with us through all of the ages. For those who will open their hearts to the Lord, He is always there. "I will never leave thee nor forsake thee." God poured out His Spirit without measure upon the earth, and that Spirit is the Spirit of Jesus. When I have the Spirit of Jesus, I have the Lord Jesus Himself, God Himself.

The Spirit of our Lord is always seeking, always inviting. It is as when God was in the Garden of Eden, seeking our first parents, Adam and Eve, whom He had made, and who had hid themselves from God. They hid from Him as though He were vicious and judgmental. But God sought them. In a world of sin and judgment and darkness, God moves. He moves in our nation. He moves in our great cities. He moves among our people. God is seeking, always caring for us even as He did in the Garden of Eden, even as He was caring in the days of Noah, even as He worked in the time of Abraham, even as He moved in the days of Moses. Through all of the centuries, God moves, seeking, searching, caring for His people.

That search is always inclusive, never exclusive. Rahab the harlot is in the genealogy of our Lord Jesus. Ruth, a Moabitess, is in the genealogy of our Lord. God sent Jonah to Nineveh, which was an ogre to the Jew. Nineveh had destroyed northern Israel. It had shut up Jerusalem like a vice. The ruthless, bitter, and hated Assyrian was a nightmare to the Jew. But God said to Jonah, "Go and preach to them." When Jonah finally preached, he did it with vengeance. "Yet forty days and Nineveh will be destroyed! Hallelujah!" They deserved the damnation of God. But the king, his noblemen, and the Assyrian people bowed before the Lord in sackcloth and ashes, and God in His mercy spared them. Jonah was disappointed that a fire did not fall and burn them up. Jonah recognized that God is long-suffering and merciful, kind, and forgiving. I try to remember that when I look at the flotsam and the jetsam of humanity, the scum of this earth. This filthy, dirty, slimy creature needs the electric chair. Another ought to be hanged! This one ought to be quartered! Then I remember, this is a man for whom Christ died. God is always inclusive, never exclusive.

The love of God is greater than the measure of man's mind, and the heart of the Eternal is most wonderfully kind! There is a God who cares about us. If you are in the fiery furnace, He is there. When Stephen was stoned, He was there. When Paul was tossed about in the awful tempest at sea, the Lord stood by Him. When John was exiled on the isle of Patmos, Jesus was there. And He is with us.

Why is it that God does not destroy Satan? Why is it that He does not forever put sin out of this world? Why is it that we live in such tribulation and trial? Why? What is the mystery of iniquity? God purposes some better thing for us. It is a secret God keeps in

His heart that we do not understand now. But the fire through which we go and the trials that we experience are part of His elective goodness for us.

One of the great doctrines that you find in the Book of Hebrews is this: Jesus, though He was the Son of God was made perfect through suffering. He learned obedience by the things that He suffered. He became our complete, able, and mighty Deliverer and Savior and sympathetic High Priest because He suffered. There is always some reason why God leads us through trials. There is an elective purpose in it all, and it is for our blessing and for our good. If you have a trial, if you have a burden, if you have a frustration, if you have a disappointment and a despair, if you have a hurt, God means through it some good thing for you. In all things God works together for good for those who love the Lord.

> When thro' fiery trials thy pathway shall lie, My grace, all-sufficient, shall be thy supply; The flame shall not hurt thee—I only design Thy dross to consume and thy gold to refine.

The providences of life that seem so cruel to us are in God's plan a part of the elective purpose by which He is fitting us for the beautiful and heavenly life that is yet to come.

GOD WILL BE SOVEREIGN OVER LIFE AND CREATION

My name is Jehovah, He says. My name is I AM THAT I AM. I AM THAT I WILL BE. Someday I will be the sole sovereign of the world. Satan no longer will dispute with us or accuse us. He will be bound and cast into the abyss forever and ever. The earth will be purged of unrighteousness, and righteousness will cover the earth as God's waters will cover the sea. In the beautiful and ultimate world that God is preparing now, there will be no more death, neither sorrow or hurt. There will be none of these things that have destroyed and ruined our lives and brought tears to our eyes and brokenness to our hearts. But we will live in His presence and with one another, world without end. We will see Him. We will be like Him. We will walk in and out before His presence with the blessing of the almighty God upon us.

Does God care for me? Does God know me? Does He know my name? Does He see me? Yes, He does. He is the One who loves, cares, sympathizes, understands, seeks, saves, forgives, helps, encourages, walks by our sides, loves us when we are un-lovely, helps us up when we fall, takes care of us in life when we cannot take care of ourselves, stands by us when we die, and receives us into glory when the time comes for us to appear before the Lord. That is our great God! Jehovah, Jesus, our Lord, our great King! Amen!

6

The Abounding Grace of God

> Moreover the law entered, that the offense might abound. But where sin abounded, grace did much more abound:
> That as sin hath reigned unto death, even so might grace reign through righteousness unto eternal life by Jesus Christ our Lord (Rom. 5:20–21).

Where sin abounded, God's grace did illimitably overflow. We think God is in heaven, where the angels bow down and worship Him. However, the Bible says that God is where sin is. God is in our cities. God is in our homes and houses. God is in our hearts. God is in our nation. God is in our world. Where sin abounds, there you will find the presence and the grace and the mercy of God.

To describe how sin "fills up" the whole earth, Paul compounds a word. He uses "illimitable" (*perisseuō*), meaning "to go beyond a fixed limit." He adds to it the Greek preposition *huper.* You cannot translate the word with an English equivalent. Where sin has "increased" or "filled up," the grace of God has gone "beyond and above the illimitable" "immeasurable" (*huperperisseuō*).

The word "grace (*charis*) is the most beautiful word in the Greek language. We use the accusative form of it in the name "Karen." *Charis* is the Greek word for "form," "beauty," and "symmetry." In architecture, statuary, painting, art, drama, and literature, the Greeks loved the beauty of form. The New Testament writers took that Greek word and applied it to God. When the Lord God left His throne of judgment, bowed down in fashion as a man, and paid the penalty for our sin, this act of unmerited favor is described as "grace." For where sin "increased" or "filled up," there did God's grace illimitably—beyond and above—overflow and abound.

SATAN WORKS THROUGH A FALLEN HUMANITY

Picture Satan in fallen humanity piling up sin and adding to it until finally it covers the face and the love of God Himself. Picture Satan in humanity with an ocean of tears and blood, drowning the mercy and the grace of our great God. Seemingly he succeeds. When you read the headlines of the papers and look at fallen humanity, you think the evil one is succeeding. When you follow the universality of the judgment of death, it looks as if Satan has accomplished his wickedness.

GOD'S GRACE IS GREATER

Where sin did abound, the grace of God did much more abound and overflow. When sin abounded in the Garden of Eden in the first Adam, the greater grace of God did much more abound in the Garden of Gethsemane in the second Adam. When sin abounded in the days of the Flood, Noah found grace in the sight of the Lord. When sin abounded in the darkness and slavery of Egypt, the grace of God did much more abound in the sacrifice of the Passover Lamb. When sin abounded in the days of the Midianites, grace did much more abound in Gideon. When sin abounded in the lives of the kings of Israel, grace did much more abound in the repentant David. When sin abounded in the awesome tragedy and sorrow of the Babylonian captivity, grace did much more abound in Daniel, Ezekiel, Ezra, and Nehemiah. When sin abounded in the days of the formal religion and the sterile, empty worship of the Sadducees and the Pharisees, grace overflowed and abounded in the face of Stephen, God's first martyr. When sin abounded in the persecution of the church, grace did much more abound in the marvelous conversion of Saul of Tarsus, who, as Paul the apostle, began to preach the faith that he once destroyed.

Sin abounds to condemn, but grace abounds to justify. Sin abounds to corrupt, but grace abounds to purify. Sin abounds to break the law and open the gates of judgment and penalty, but grace abounds to heal the breach. Sin abounds to imprison in death and darkness, but grace abounds to set the captives free. Sin abounds to consume the soul and life, but grace abounds to abrogate the flame, to quench the fire. Sin abounds to slay and to destroy, but grace abounds to bestow life and light and glory. "For the wages of sin is death; but the gift [grace] of God is eternal life" (Rom. 6:23).

WHAT GOD HAS DONE FOR US

Paul writes of this in a marvelous and glorious way. Salvation is a gift of God. It is something God does for us. Paul describes this marvelous grace of God by using five aorist participles in 2 Timothy 1:9–10. The English language does not have an aorist tense. This tense refers to something done at a point in time—something that is done, past, and accomplished.

(1) "God hath *saved* [*sosantos* from root meaning 'to deliver' or 'to save'] us."
(2) "God hath *called* [*kalesantos* from root meaning 'to call'] us."
(3) "God hath *given* [*dotheisan* from root meaning 'to give' or 'to bestow'] us grace in Christ Jesus."
(4) "The Lord hath *abolished* [*katargesantos* from a root meaning 'to render useless,' 'to annul,' 'to abrogate'] death."
(5) "He hath *brought* [*photisantos* from a root meaning 'to reveal' or 'to bring to light,' from which our 'photograph' comes] life and immortality to light."

All five of these verbs refer to something God has already done. He has saved us; He has called us; He has given us His grace in Christ Jesus; He has abolished death; He has brought life and immortality to light. What a marvelous and wondrous thing God has done for us! It is His gift to us.

Our deliverance and our salvation—He does it all! It is His work from start to finish. The second chapter of Jonah closes with the prophet's prayer as he is in the belly of the great fish (2:9). He faces inevitable death. He cannot save himself. In his prayer, he affirms that "Salvation is of the LORD." God has to do it. Jonah could not have saved himself. God had to save him.

The same doctrine is avowed by the apostle Paul in Titus 3:5:

Not by works of righteousness which we have done, but according to his mercy he saved us, by the washing of regeneration, and renewing of the Holy Ghost.

We cannot save ourselves. It is the work of God. Creation cannot create itself. God has to do it. Only in the fuzzy-minded thinking and in the aberration of a pseudoscientist does something ever come out of nothing. Only in the demented mind does inanimate matter create personality and mind and intelligence. Rather, God has to create. Creation cannot create itself.

A temple cannot build itself; an architect, a contractor, and a builder have to raise it. The dead cannot raise themselves; they cannot bring themselves to life and immortality. Neither can the lost sinner save himself. God has to do it for him. Good works do not avail. All of our righteousnesses are as filthy rags. Grace, mercy, resurrection, forgiveness, salvation, and deliverance come from God's mighty hands. God saves us! Our good works, our songs, and our praises are in thanksgiving for what the Lord has done for us.

This marvelous work of grace that God has wrought in our souls is not partial or fragmented; it is wholly and completely done in Christ. It is not a piece of salvation or a gesture toward deliverance. It is not a suggestion of what God is able to do. It is a work wholly, completely, and marvelously finished by our Lord. What a marvelous thing God has done for us in saving us! It is not partly done but wholly done. It is not something in which He has done some and we have done some. But all of it is of God through His grace. Any man who thinks that he is saved partly by trusting Jesus and partly by his own good works has never trusted Jesus.

Salvation is wholly of God. It is as if a man were to go down to the bank, holding in his hand a deposit. He stands at the teller's cage and says, "I want to deposit this money, but I do not trust you with it. So I am going to let you hold half of it on that end and I am going to hold the other half on this end." The teller would look at that man and say, "I must have on my hands a sheer, unadulterated idiot!" I either trust the bank or I do not trust the bank. I make the deposit or I do not make the deposit. It is one or the other.

A man may go to the airport to take a plane ride, and he might say, "I do not trust this thing; so when I fly, I am going to keep one foot on the ground." That man is not going to fly! I think one of the craziest things I ever heard was about the man who got off a plane and said, "But I did not put my whole weight down!" I either trust or I do not trust. I either fly or I do not fly. I take off or I stay on the ground.

It is exactly that way with our blessed Lord. I either trust Him or I do not. It is not partly of Him and the rest of me. It is completely of Him. Any good that I might do is not a cause of my salvation; it is a consequence of my salvation. My life is to be given to the praise, love, worship, and adoration of the great, wonderful God whose grace lifted me out of death into the light of the immortality of His love and mercy. Our lives are just to praise the Lord for what He has done for us in His goodness and in His grace. There is no place for confessional booths, beads, purgatories, or ablutions. It is all of God.

The gospel of the world is, "Work and strive and try to do good and you will be saved." But the gospel of the Son of God is this, "Look and live. It is recorded in His Word, Hallelujah! It is only that you look and live." The gospel of salvation is always "wash and be clean."

> What can wash away my sin?
> Nothing but the blood of Jesus;
> What can make me whole again?
> Nothing but the blood of Jesus.
> O! precious is the flow
> That makes me white as snow;
> No other fount I know,
> Nothing but the blood of Jesus.

The gospel of the grace of the Son of God is always, "Believe and be saved."

In my studying I came across this poem. It was written years ago by a Christian in an old-fashioned way.

> Until I saw the blood
> 'Twas hell my soul was fearing.
> And dark and dreary in my eyes
>   the future was appearing,
> While conscience told its tale of sin
> And caused a weight of woe within.
>
> But when I saw the blood
>   and looked at Him who shed it,

My right to peace was seen at once,
    and I with transport read it.
I found myself to God brought nigh
And "victory" became my cry.
My joy was in the blood
    the news of which had told me,
That spotless as the Lamb of God
    my Father could behold me.
And all my boast was in His name
Through whom this great salvation came.

God did it! It is a gift of God. It is of grace, unmerited favor, lest, as Paul wrote, any man should boast. That is, lest any man should say, "I did it. All praise to me." This marvelous gift of God is something the Lord has wrought for us. He did it!

THE MARVELOUS SALVATION IN CHRIST

In this last century there was a famous infidel, who was also one of the greatest orators America has ever produced. His name was Robert G. Ingersoll. He went all over the United States lecturing on atheism. In one of his brilliant lectures he said,

> I do not believe in forgiveness. If I rob Smith and afterward I get forgiveness, how does that help Smith? If I cover some poor girl with the leprosy of some imputed crime and she withers away like a blighted flower and afterwards I get forgiveness, how does that help her? Even if there is another world—we have got to settle. . . . No forgiveness; eternal, inexorable, everlasting justice, that is what I believe in.

That is right! The infidel was absolutely right. An eternal, everlasting justice is what he and all of the rest of us shall inexorably and inevitably face. The world is one vast, illimitable cemetery in which men such as these are paying the penalty of death for sin and breaking the law of God.

There is a great high wall and in it is a massive iron gate. Behind that wall and behind that iron gate is the agonizing of all humanity, facing death and judgment and going down to the grave in tears and indescribable sorrow. Justice stands at the gate to guard it. He holds the keys in his hand. Before that gate Mercy weeps. She cries, saying to Justice: "Open those iron bars and let me enter in that I may wipe away their tears and assuage their sorrow and bring comfort and hope to their hearts. Open the gate and let me enter in."

Justice replies to weeping Mercy: "No. They have broken the law, and the wages of the breaking of the law is death. Either they die or Justice dies. Justice must be administered." So says the infidel; so says Justice.

An emissary of angels passing by on a celestial mission looked on that tragic scene and saw Mercy weeping at the iron gate of Justice. The angels paused and said to Mercy, "Why do you weep?"

She replied: "Because I cannot enter. I cannot help in sorrow or in death. I can only weep. Justice will not open the door and Justice will not let me in."

Justice in defense of himself said to the emissary of ambassadorial angels: "Correct, they have broken the law and the law must be honored and the penalty must be paid. Either they die or Justice dies."

Upon that there stepped forth from the band of angels one in form and fashion like unto the Son of God. He came up to Justice and said, "What are your terms?"

Justice replied, "They have broken the law. If the law is not observed, the universe will crumble. All law must be commanded with a penalty."

The law of gravity—break it and you will pay a penalty. The law of fire—break it and you will pay a penalty. The law of explosive motion—break it and you will pay a penalty. The universe is governed by law, and law is law because it is enforced with a penalty.

Moral law is enforced. The wages of sin is death, and the soul that sins shall die. A penalty has been incurred. The claim must be satisfied. The law must be honored. The debt must be paid.

The Lord Jesus replied to Justice, "If I pay the debt, if I satisfy the claim, will they go free?"

Justice replied, "If you pay the debt. . . ."

And then I remembered the riches of glory in Christ Jesus. He is able.

The Lord said, "If I satisfy the claim. . . ."

And then I remembered reading, "God shall see of the travail of his soul and shall be satisfied."

"If I pay the debt and if I satisfy the claims, can they go free?"

Justice replies, "I will open the gate."

On a hill at a set time, Mercy and Justice stand waiting. That hill is called Golgotha, "the place of a skull," or in Latin, "Calvary." That moment has been in type since the beginning of creation. Every lamb that was slain, every sacrifice that was offered, every drop of blood poured out before the Lord is a type of that day. In all of the prophecies of grace, God laid upon Him the iniquity of us all that day (Is. 53:6). At the exact time prophesied by Daniel the prophet in the sixty-ninth week, Justice said to Mercy, "Where is the Lamb of God?"

Mercy replied, "Behold, He cometh, bearing a cross, followed by His weeping church."

The Son of God came up that hill to Justice. Justice has in his hand the ordinances and the commandments and the laws and the penalties and the judgments against us. The Lord took them from the hand of Justice, and they were nailed to the cross.

Justice spoke to Death and said, "Come, and consume this sacrifice." Death replied: "I come. After I consume the sacrifice I will slay and consume the whole world." And Death descended upon the sacrifice of the Son of God and consumed the ordinances and the laws and the penalties and the judgments and consumed His humanity and He died!

But when Death touched the deity of the Son of God, His purity and His holiness, it was as though he had touched a bolt of a wire of a billion powers! Death itself was consumed! It expired there that day on the cross. The darkness burst into light, and the very earth that shook opened the graves of the dead! On a Sabbath morning on the first day of the week, the Son of God came forth triumphant and victorious!

When Mercy looked upon the sight, she cried with rejoicing and gladness. When Grace looked upon that sight, she overflowed in abounding love. Proclaim throughout the world deliverance and salvation, for the great iron gate was opened wide, and God's people poured forth in everlasting praise! Sin received its mortal blow. Death and hell were cast into the lake of fire, and God's redeemed and rejoicing people sang the praises of Him who liveth forever and ever! "Worthy is the Lamb that was slain to receive power, and riches, and wisdom, and strength, and honor, and glory, and blessing" (Rev. 5:12). For He has redeemed us by His blood unto God, and we shall reign forever and ever. And the four cherubim said, "Amen!" And the four and twenty elders fell down and worshiped Him who lives forever and forever!

It is of God. He does it. It is of grace. It is in His love and mercy. Bound by death and in iron chains, we are helpless in trespasses and in sins. Immortality and resurrection walk among the tombs of the dead. The trumpet sounds, the archangel's voice is heard, and God's redeemed people will be raised in glory to praise our wonderful Lord forever and ever and ever! Amen.

That is our worship and our life. We do not work and strive in order that we may save ourselves. But we gather in songs, in prayer, in worship, in adoration, and in praise, thanking God for what Jesus has done for us. For where sin abounded, God's grace did much more abound.

7

The Unfathomable Mystery of the Trinity

The grace of the Lord Jesus Christ, and the love of God, and the communion of the Holy Ghost be with you all. Amen (2 Cor. 13:14).

The Trinity is named in this letter Paul wrote to the Corinthians. Here is a trinitarian, tripersonality benediction: "The *grace* of the Lord Jesus, the *love* of God, and the *communion* of the Holy Ghost"—the triune God. The unfathomable mystery of the Trinity—not that this is the only unfathomable mystery—just that this unfathomable mystery reaches to infinity.

We live in the midst of inexplicable mystery. We ourselves are a constituent part of it. There is no more nonunderstandable, inexplicable, unfathomable mystery than you yourself. Sometimes the Bible, the Lord Jesus, and the apostle Paul will speak of a man as being a dichotomy. The Bible will refer to us as a *psuche* and a *soma,* a "soul" and a "body." Now how could they be together, intermingled and comingled in one you? How do spirit and materiality, corporeality, mix together?

Sometimes the Bible, and especially the apostle Paul, will refer to us as a trichotomy. Paul will refer to us as a material, physical being (*somatikos*). He will also refer to us as a thinking, feeling being (*psuchekos*). He will also refer to us as a spiritual being, sensitive to the spirit of God (*pneumatikos*).

We are in one sense a unity, a personality. We are also in another sense a plurality, a trinity—a *soma,* a *psuche,* and a *pneuma.* How do you put all of that together in one you? How

68

could mind, spirit, and will influence matter? How does this Trinity move and breathe and live in us? How am I both spirit (invisible and immaterial) and body (corporeal and physical)? Nobody knows. Nobody will ever know. There are limits to human understanding. In fact, we are limited in every area of our understanding. All we do is look, see, and observe. We do not understand anything.

If this is true, how much more infinitely is it inexplicable and unfathomable when we reach toward the infinitude of the mystery of the sacred Trinity in the godhead.

In reading the life of Augustine, I note that one day when he was walking along the seashore, he saw a little boy digging a trench in the sand. He walked over to the lad and asked him what he was doing. The little fellow replied, "Sir, I am making a trench." "Why are you doing it?" said Augustine. The little lad replied, "I am going to empty the sea into my trench." This great thinker, the greatest of the Latin Fathers, continued his walk and mused: "So the lad thinks that he is going to empty the sea into the little trench he has made in the sand. Sometimes we are like that. We propose to encompass the infinitude of God in the small limits of our mind."

It cannot be achieved; it is impossible. We cannot understand or explain even the works of God. Where did the sun come from? Who made it? How did we get here? Who made us? How are we made? We cannot understand even the phenomena of the works of God all around us—the mud, the muck, and the mire that can burst into these beautiful and flaming flowers. How much less can we understand the great mystery of God Himself! In the order of creation, the higher the order, the more complex and inexplicable it becomes. Begin with a rock or a clod, then rise to a tree or a plant, then rise upward to an animal, then rise upward to a man, and finally rise upward to God. The infinite, unfathomable mystery of the Trinity!

GOD REVEALS HIMSELF TO US AS TRIPERSONALITY

In the revelation of God in His Word, He reveals Himself to us as tripersonality, one in three, and three in one. All are co-equal, coeternal, one in essence, three in subsistence.

God is personality. He is somebody. He reveals Himself as a person. He speaks, He thinks, He acts, He communicates, He feels. That is God. We are verbal creatures, and God communicates to us in words, language, thought. The self-disclosure of God is always personal. He is not a philosophical principle. He is not an academician's abstraction. He is not a barren, sterile, impersonal first cause. God is somebody, and He reveals Himself to us as the God of Abraham, of Isaac, of Jacob, of David, and of Isaiah, the God whose personal name in the Old Testament is Jehovah, *Yahweh.* His name in the New Testament is *Iesous,* Jesus, Savior, our Lord.

In the Bible, Abraham is labeled as a friend of God, not a friend of an abstract principle but a friend of God. The same Holy Scriptures say that Moses spoke to God as a man would speak to a friend, face to face. God in the Bible is personal.

In the Holy Scriptures, He reveals Himself as tripersonal. There are three eternal, coequal distinctions in the Godhead. All through the Bible, beginning at the first verse of the first chapter of the first book to the last benediction, that Trinity, the tripersonality in the Godhead, is always apparent, ever present, always self-disclosed and revealed.

THE TRINITY IN THE OLD TESTAMENT

We shall look first at the Trinity, the self-disclosure of God in tripersonality in the Old Testament Scriptures.

> In the beginning God created the heaven and the earth.
> And the earth was without form, and void; and darkness was upon the face of the deep. And the Spirit of God moved upon the face of the waters.
> And God said, Let us make man in our image, after our likeness. . . . (Gen. 1:1, 2, 26a).

There is a plurality in God. In the first syllables of the first verse He is introduced to us as a plurality. The singular form of the word for God is *El.* You find it in a thousand combinations in the Old Testament Scriptures. The plural is *Elohim,* which is the form used in Genesis 1.

In this first chapter of Genesis, that word *Elohim* is used thirty-two times. In the books of Moses, *Elohim* is used more than five hundred times. In the Old Testament Scriptures *Elohim* is used more than five thousand times. In all thirty-two times in the first chapter of Genesis, in all of the more than five hundred times in the writings of Moses, and in all of the more than five thousand times in the Old Testament, without exception *Elohim* is used with a singular verb. *Elohim,* plural, referring to the majesty and abounding marvel and mystery of God, appears with the singular verb. That is God.

The second distinction in the godhead introduced to us is the Spirit of God. "The Spirit of God moved upon the face of the waters." The moving of the Spirit of God is presented all through the Old Testament Scriptures. The Spirit came upon Bezaleel and Aholiab that they might contrive the beautiful artifacts, furniture, accouterments, and embellishments of the holy tabernacle where God was worshiped. The Spirit of God came upon David, Israel's sweet psalmist and singer. The Spirit of God left Saul, and an evil spirit troubled him. Zechariah, the prophet, said, "Not by might, nor by power, but by my Spirit, said the LORD" (Zech. 4:6). A tripersonality, eternal distinctions in the godhead—*Elohim,* God; *Ruach,* the Spirit of God. "Let us make man in *our* image, and after *our* likeness."

There is another somebody, another person who appears all through the Old Testament. He is called the Angel of God or the Angel of the Presence, and He is always there.

In Genesis 22 we find the moving, marvelous story of the offering up of Isaac on Mt. Moriah. As Abraham raised his hand to plunge the knife into the heart of his only begotten son of promise by Sarah, a voice spoke to Abraham, and this is the story:

> And the angel of the LORD called unto Abraham out of heaven the second time,
> And said, By myself have I sworn, saith the LORD, for because thou hast done this thing, and hast not withheld thy son, thine only son:
> That in blessing I will bless thee, and in multiplying I will multiply thy seed as the stars of the heaven . . .
> And in thy seed shall all of the nations of the earth be blessed . . . (Gen. 22:15–18).

Who was that angel of the Lord who spoke to Abraham and said, "By myself have I sworn, saith the LORD. . . . That in blessing I will bless thee . . ."?

Or again in Genesis 31, the angel of the Lord spoke unto Jacob, "I am the God of Bethel. . . ." Who was that angel of the Lord who spoke thus to Israel?

In Exodus 3 we read that Moses was keeping his father-in-law Jethro's flock on the back side of the desert. During the day he saw a bush burning unconsumed, and he turned aside to see why the bush had not been consumed. When God saw that he turned aside, He spoke unto Moses out of the flaming bush saying, "I am the God of . . . Abraham, the God of Isaac, and the God of Jacob" (Ex. 3:6a). Who was this angel of the Lord who spoke to Moses out of the flame and the fire?

Look at the story of Joshua and the conquest of Canaan. Having crossed the Jordan and surrounded Jericho, Joshua saw standing before him a warrior with a sword in his hand.

> Joshua went unto him, and said unto him, Art thou for us, or for our adversaries?
>
> And he said, Nay; but as captain of the host of the LORD am I now come. And Joshua fell on his face to the earth, and did worship, and said unto him, What saith my lord unto his servant?
>
> And the captain of the LORD'S host said unto Joshua, Loose thy shoe from off thy foot; for the place whereon thou standest is holy (Josh. 5:13b–15).

Who was that warrior who appeared before Joshua and announced himself as being captain of the host of the people of God?

In that incomparable story in Daniel 3, the furnace was heated seven times hotter, and the three Hebrew children were thrown in it.

> Then Nebuchadnezzar the king was astonished, and rose up in haste, and spake, and said unto his counselors, Did not we cast three men bound into the midst of the fire? They answered and said unto the king, True, O king.
>
> He answered and said, Lo, I see four men loose, walking in the midst of the fire, and they have no hurt; and the form of the fourth is like the Son of God (Dan. 3:24–25).

Who was that in the fire with them?

All through the Old Testament Scriptures He appears. You can call it an epiphany, an appearance of God. You can call it a Christophany, the preincarnate presence of Jesus our Lord. The three are always in the Old Testament: *Elohim*—God; *Ruach*—the Spirit of God; and the angel of His presence, whom we know as Jesus our Lord. In the Old Testament God reveals and discloses Himself as a triune personality with eternal distinctions within the godhead.

The Unfathomable Mystery of the Trinity

When we turn to the New Testament, the same marvelous, mysterious, unfathomable revelation and self-disclosure of God is made. Just as in the Old Testament, so in the New Testament is there a trinity in the personality of God.

In the first chapter of the Gospel of Matthew, the Spirit of God has conceived a child in the womb of the virgin Mary.

> Behold the angel of the Lord appeared unto him in a dream, saying, Joseph, thou son of David, fear not to take unto thee Mary thy wife: for that which is conceived in her is of the Holy Ghost.
>
> And she shall bring forth a son, and thou shalt call his name JESUS: for he shall save his people from their sins.
>
> Now all this was done, that it might be fulfilled which was spoken of the Lord by the prophet, saying,
>
> Behold, a virgin shall be with child, and shall bring forth a son, and they shall call his name Immanuel, which being interpreted, is God with us (Matt. 1:20b–23).

All three persons are in those verses: God, our Father; the Holy Spirit, who wrought conception in the womb of Mary; and Joshua, Savior, Jesus, who will save His people from their sins, being Immanuel, God with us.

In the beginning of the messianic ministry of Jesus the three are named together.

> And Jesus, when he was baptized, went up straightway out of the water: and, lo, the heavens were opened unto him, and he saw the Spirit of God descending like a dove, and lighting upon him:
>
> And lo a voice from heaven, saying, This is my beloved Son, in whom I am well pleased (Matt. 3:16–17).

This is the triunity in God's personality.

The Book closes like that. As His messianic ministry begins, so it consummates in that same Trinity.

> Go ye therefore, and teach all nations, baptizing them in the name [singular] of [I have three names; God has three names] the Father, and of the Son, and of the Holy Ghost (Matt. 28:19–20).

Throughout all of the New Testament the Trinity is presented. The self-disclosure of God is made over and over again. You will find that Trinity named in these Scriptures: Luke 1:35; John 14:26; 15:26; 2 Corinthians 13:14; Galatians 4:6; 1 Peter 1:2; Jude 20–21; Revelation 1:4–6. I went through the Book of Ephesians and found the three names in that book alone in all of these verses: Ephesians 1:17; 2:18; 3:14-16; 4:4-7; 5:18-20; 6:17-23. In the beautiful text in 2 Corinthians 13:14, we see the three names,

> The grace of the Lord Jesus Christ, and the love of God, and the communion of the Holy Ghost, be with you all. Amen.

Woven throughout the entire New Testament is the self-disclosure of God as a tripersonality: God, our Father; God, our Savior, and God, the Holy Spirit, moving in our souls.

AN AMAZING DISCOVERY

In my studying I came across one of the most amazing things I have ever found in the Bible. Wherever the three personalities of the Trinity are presented together, and they stand together all through the Bible, without exception it is always in redemptive blessing, in merciful loving-kindness, in salvation, and deliverance. There is no exception to that.

Sometimes when the Father is presented alone, it is in a fury of judgment, such as the Father was clothed in thunder and lightning and judgment as He delivered the commandments on the top of Mt. Sinai. The very mountains shook with the darkness of the flame and the fire! The presentation of God as the judge of all the earth is awesome!

Consider the Lord Jesus Christ in His address at the temple during the last week of His life. He spoke of Himself as being the stone of stumbling, and if the stone falls upon a man it will grind to powder (Matt. 21:44)! The picture of Jesus as a judge of men who reject Him and disown Him is awesome!

Or take again the appearance of the third person in the Trinity by Himself.

> Wherefore I say unto you, All manner of sin and blasphemy shall be forgiven unto men: but the blasphemy against the Holy Ghost shall not be forgiven unto men.
> And whosoever speaketh a word against the Son of man, it shall be forgiven him: but whosoever speaketh against the Holy Ghost, it shall not be forgiven him, neither in this world, neither in the world to come (Matt. 12:31-32).

The man who blasphemes the Holy Spirit has committed an unpardonable and unforgivable sin. It is awesome!

But when all three of them appear together, when they are

revealed together, without exception in the Bible, it is always in mercy, grace, loving-kindness, and in salvation.

Look at two passages—one in the Old Testament and one in the New Testament.

> I will mention the loving-kindnesses of the LORD, and the praises of the LORD, according to all that the LORD hath bestowed on us, and the great goodness toward the house of Israel, which he hath bestowed on them according to his mercies, and according to the multitude of his loving-kindnesses.
>
> For he said, Surely they are my people, children that will not lie: so he was their Savior.
>
> In all their affliction he was afflicted, and the angel of his presence saved them: in his love and in his pity he redeemed them; and he bare them, and carried them all the days of old (Is. 63:7–10).

What a beautiful picture of the great triune God!

In this New Testament passage the Trinity is presented again.

> John to the seven churches which are in Asia: Grace be unto you, and peace, from him which is, and which was, and which is to come; [God, the Father] and from the seven Spirits which are before his throne; [The word seven means the plenitude, the grace and mercy of the Spirit of God.]
>
> And from Jesus Christ [the second person of the Trinity], who is the faithful witness, and the first begotten of the dead, and the prince of the kings of the earth. Unto him that loved us, and washed us from our sins in his own blood,
>
> And hath made us kings and priests unto God and his Father; to him be glory and dominion for ever and ever. Amen (Rev. 1:4–6).

Wherever the three are presented together in the Bible, it is always in loving-kindness, in tender mercy, in redemptive love and deliverance.

GOD REVEALS HIMSELF IN HUMAN EXPERIENCE

We know God in our human experience as tripersonality: God the Father, transcendent above all; God the Son, eminent in all; and God the Holy Spirit, inherent in all. Our experience is trinitarian. God is holy. How could a sinful man ever approach the divine holiness of God? No man can even see His face and live. We cannot even look at the sun which is one of the small creations of His hands, much less could we look into the face of the glory of God Himself, the transcendent God.

We approach our great God in our Lord's loving-kindness

and favor and redemptive love, in His blood of sacrifice that covers our sins and washes the stain out of our souls. We approach God in Christ. We are creatures for whom He died. We are sinners whom He saved. We know God only as Jesus opens the door that we might approach His presence.

And the Spirit of God moves in our hearts thus to bring Him to us in loving salvation. When I preach, the Spirit of God is in the hearts of my listeners, and He confirms the witness of the Word by the moving in their souls. Thus are we brought to the great heavenly Father. We are invited to come boldly, sinners as we are, unworthy as we are. We are to come boldly that we might find grace to help in time of need.

We experience the salvation of God in that trinitarian form. Jesus died for us. He covered our sins in His own sacrifice and love. The Holy Spirit takes the message of Jesus and woos and pulls in our hearts, and we come before God in His name, in His grace. That is the way we were saved, and that is the way we live as Christians.

That is the way we pray. Abraham said, "Behold, I have taken upon myself to speak unto thee, I who am but dust and ashes." Unworthy as we are, we come before God in the name of Jesus; i.e., we ground our hope and faith in His righteousness, in His loving mercy. We plead in Jesus' name. And we come moved by the Spirit of God in our hearts. Were it not for the Spirit of God, we would never come; we would never trust; we would never believe; we would never pray. It is the moving Spirit of God that leads us to the Lord. In our salvation and in our daily living all three persons of the Godhead have a beautiful part.

Let me sum up one other truth. Whenever anyone departs from the revelation of God as a tripersonality, he immediately falls into a barren and sterile faith without comfort and without hope.

That is true with regard to Jesus our Lord. If we deny the Trinity, then Jesus is just another man, and He died as all other men have died and is in a grave somewhere as all other men are in their graves. He could not perfectly represent to us the Father because He is just another man. We have no assurance. He does not hear our prayers. He does not comfort our souls. He does not have any word of grace and salvation. He cannot pardon our sins. He cannot sustain and keep us. He is a man as all other men.

On the other hand, we can accept the revelation of God that Jesus is the great wonderful Savior, the second person of the Trinity, who reveals to us our Lord God and who brings us in salvation into His saving presence. Others may scoff or scorn that we worship a creature, a man. But this man Jesus is revealed to us as God. He represents God in the flesh. If I want to know God, He is God. If I want to see God, I look at Him. If I want to worship God, I worship Him.

In the ruins of ancient Rome a caricature is scratched on a wall of the Palatine palace. It is a picture, rude and crude, of a man with the head of an ass nailed to a cross. In front of the ass-headed man nailed to the cross is a crude picture of a man kneeling in worship. Underneath is the caption scribbled in incorrect Greek, "Alexamenos adores his god." That was the attitude of the scornful, contemptuous Greek and Roman in the first Christian century. But by the side of Alexamenos, we also would kneel before that cross, numbered among those who believe that in Christ we have the full-orbed revelation of God. Thus we believe in the Holy Spirit, and thus we believe in the infallible and inerrant Scriptures that have revealed to us this tripersonality of God, and thus we are brought to worship the true God of heaven and earth.

Whenever men worship an inferior God, no matter what you call it, the man is debased and degraded. There is no exception to it in history. Whether the god that is worshiped is made out of stone, gold, silver, or any kind of an idolatrous image, the worship is a degrading thing to the man who bows before it. The same is true in modern life. When men today worship an inferior god such as the deification of man called Humanism, or whether they worship pleasure, fortune, ambition, fame, or success, whatever it is to which they give their lives, the man in his soul and in his life is debased and degraded.

When a man worships the true God, when he bows before the Lord Jesus Christ, when he accepts in his heart the testimony of the Holy Spirit who points to the saving grace of Jesus, the man is exalted, he is lifted up, he is edified. Everything that concerns his life is sanctified and made heavenly and holy.

There is one God and His name is God our Father, and God our Savior, and God in our souls—the moving grace and witness of the Holy Spirit. Amen.

8

The Miracle of God's Incarnation

The angel Gabriel was sent to Mary, a virgin girl in Nazareth. The angel made this announcement to her:

> And, behold, thou shalt conceive in thy womb, and bring forth a son, and shalt call his name Jesus [*Joshua*, Hebrew, and *Iesus*, Greek. In every language, the word means "Savior" or "Jehovah saves"].
> He shall be great, and shall be called the Son of the Highest: and the Lord God shall give unto him the throne of his father David:
> And he shall reign over the house of Jacob for ever; and of his kingdom there shall be no end (Luke 1:31–33).

From the beginning of this announcement, the preaching of the Christian faith has literally been interdicted, denied, and abused. There has not been anything evil and vicious that could be said about the Christian faith that has not been said.

There is a possible repercussion, an overtone of that violent interdiction, when Jesus was questioned by His accusers in John 8:19, "They said unto him, Where is thy Father?"

In the days of the sainted apostle John, who was pastor in Ephesus in his old age, there was a gnostic named Cerinthus. He taught that Jesus was born by natural generation from Joseph and Mary and that the emanation, i.e., the messianic Spirit from heaven, came upon Jesus at His baptism and then left Him at His crucifixion. Cerinthus began with a denial of the Incarnation and the Virgin Birth.

In the Talmud, the oral tradition of the Jews that has been carried down through the generations, there are stories that suggest immoral illegitimacy in the birth of Christ. In those stories, a Roman officer named Panthera supposedly lived with a Jewish girl named Mary in Nazareth. Into that illegitmate union the child called Jesus was supposedly born. Those stories of illegitimacy have continued through the years.

Celsus, a brilliant and able antagonist of the second century, repeated those stories. Voltaire, the tremendously gifted French philosopher and infidel, repeated those same Talmudic slurs in the eighteenth century. Even in this last century, Tolstoy, the incomparable Russian author and novelist, repeated them.

In our day there are two tremendous focuses of battle and confrontation:

(1) The inspiration of the Holy Scriptures. That battle rages world without end. In every denomination and even now among our own Southern Baptists, the battle rages over whether or not the Bible is the Word of God or whether it was written by men as they tried to interpret the meaning of God. Is it the infallible revelation of God, or is it man's attempt to write what he thinks God is? That is the first focus of war in the theological world.

(2) The other battleground concerns the Virgin Birth. Bitterly and continually the doctrine of the Virgin Birth is attacked by the critics of the Bible. Matthew Arnold, one of the tremendous literary figures of England, said: "I do not believe in the virgin birth, for that would imply miracle and I do not believe in miracles. Miracles do not happen."

A rationalistic higher critic named Loof wrote, "I think it the duty of truthfulness to state openly that the virgin birth arose out of fabulous [fictitious] tradition." Indeed, it may be forensically interesting among infidels for a man to say: "I do not believe in the virgin birth. I think it is fictitious. I do not believe in the inspiration of the Bible, and I do not believe it is the infallible Word of God. These stories in the Bible are just manufactured out of somebody's wild, illimitable, ungovernable imagination." But what are you going to do about explaining some of the great facts of human life in history?

For example, the greatest single fact that I know in human history is the fact of Jesus Christ. I do not know another fact comparable to it. I think you can explain the lives of Alexander the Great, Julius Caesar, or Napoleon Bonaparte. I think you can explain the genius of Shakespeare, Homer, or Dante. I think you can understand the scientific prowess that lies behind a Thomas Alva Edison or an Albert Einstein. I think they are in human categories and belong to human denominators. But I do not know how any man in any age is able to explain the unique, towering personality of Jesus the Christ. How do you do it? There is something about Him that is the great unlike.

A rationalist named Schmidt once wrote:

> Jesus is inexplicable psychologically, casually, or by evolutionary development. Something derived creatively from God is necessary to explain the life and consciousness of Jesus.

To compare the greatest men of the earth, like an Alexander or a Caesar or a Shakespeare, with Jesus is like comparing a grain of dust to the whole universe, like comparing a molehill to Mount Everest in the Himalayas! I repeat: I do not think there is fact in human history like the fact of Jesus Christ—there has been and is none like Him. How do you explain Him? Where did He come from?

There are those who worship at the shrine of pseudoscience. They seek to find some natural, phenomenal explanation to all of the "miracles" in the Bible. They do it sometimes ingeniously.

Here is an example of such ingenuity. The Bible describes the marvelous miracle of the deliverance of the children of Israel at the Red Sea. They went through with the waters piled up on either side of them. Then when Pharaoh's army tried to follow after them, God let the waters go back again and drowned Pharaoh's army. That is what the Bible says. But these so-called scientists and critics say: "That was not the Red Sea. It was the Reed Sea, and the water was about three inches deep. It did not even come up to their ankles. The children of Israel just walked through." That is a fine explanation except when it comes to drowning Pharaoh's army in three inches of water!

Let us take another. The higher critics, explaining away the Bible and its supernatural, miraculous element, relate the account of Elijah's praying down fire on Mt. Carmel as being just a bolt of lightning that happened to fall and consume the sacrifice at that particular moment—just an ordinary, coincidental phenomenon. In like manner they say that the resurrection of Christ was a mental aberration—nothing more than hallucination. Those bearing testimony of the risen Lord were actually duped; they just thought that they saw Jesus raised from among the dead.

The same type of mentality that seeks some kind of natural, phenomenal explanation for the miracles of the Bible also explains away the Virgin Birth. These unbelieving intellectuals say that there is a thing called parthenogenesis. That is, there are fungi and algae and plant lice that self-fertilize from spores. They do not need male and female, they just self-fertilize from spores. They hold that Mary just self-fertilized like a plant louse, like a fungus, like an alga.

Let us take another one. At the gathering of a theological society, a teacher read a paper discussing the Virgin Birth. A professor in the university stood up and offered a scientific explanation for the phenomenon of Mary's giving birth to the child. He said that female rabbits have been known to be shocked into conception without a male and that Mary may well have been shocked into conception by the startling appearance and announcement of the angel Gabriel. That theory deserves a reward of some kind for its ingenuity! Those things are just unimaginable to me. To place Mary in the category of a plant louse or an alga or a fungus or a shocked rabbit is beyond me!

Some say that the Virgin Birth is not a part of the Bible. But wherever there is a manuscript of the Bible, the Virgin Birth is in it. As far back as these ancient autographs can be traced, in every version, this is woven into the Word of God.

Of course, there are others who compare the phenomenal and miraculous births in the Greek and Roman mythologies to the birth of Christ. They say this is just another one of those mythological stories about somebody who is supposed to be great. Alexander the Great, for example, is no longer the son of Philip of Macedon, but the offspring of a serpent who cohabited with his mother. The mother of Augustus Caesar went to sleep in the temple of Apollo, and Apollo transformed himself into a serpent (I do not know why they liked those serpents), and Augustus Octavius Caesar was born.

In the story of Hercules, Alcmene is the daughter of Electryon (the Brilliant), son of Perseus. While her husband was away, Jupiter transformed himself into the likeness of her husband and Hercules was born. And when Juno the wife of Jupiter Jove heard of it, she sent two enormous pythons to destroy the baby. The baby Hercules seized one python with one hand and the other python with the other hand, and then strangled them to death.

Or look at the mythological story of the birth and life of Achilles. Peleus was the king of Thessaly, and he cohabited with Thetis who was a sea nymph, and out of that union Achilles was born. Thetis took Achilles and dipped him in the River Styx to make him immortal, but she held him by his heels, which left him vulnerable only at that spot. In the Trojan War, Paris of Troy took a poisoned arrow and shot Achilles in the heel and he died.

A tradition outside of Greek-Roman mythology is the story of Gautama the Buddha. For two or three hundred years after Gautama, there were no stories about his birth. Then miracle stories began to circulate about how he came into the world. His mother had a dream, and she saw an enormous elephant with six tusks. The great elephant forced himself into the side of the mother, and Gautama the Buddha, "the Enlightened One," was born.

There are two observations to be made about these stories: (1) They are all plainly and flagrantly and manifestly manufactured. They are fictitious. (2) Not one of them has to do with a virgin birth. They have no theological meaning. We are now back from where we started. How do you explain the incomparable, towering character and personality of Jesus Christ? From where did He come? We have a certain and reasonable and God-honored answer.

THE BIRTH OF CHRIST IS A WORK OF THE HOLY SPIRIT

Christ Jesus is a fashioning, a making, a creation of the Holy Spirit of God. The Holy Spirit fashioned a body for the incarnate Savior of the world. God did it. In that marvelous passage in Luke 1, the angel Gabriel said to Mary:

> The Holy Ghost shall come upon thee, and the power of the Highest shall overshadow thee: therefore also that holy thing which shall be born of thee shall be called the Son of God (Luke 1:35).

His birth was the work of the Holy Spirit.

It is a remarkable thing that at the beginning of the life of our Lord the creative and fashioning work of the Holy Spirit of God is present, and at the end of His life His resurrection is also described as the work of the Holy Spirit of God (Rom. 1:4). The Spirit of God created the body in the womb of Mary, and the Holy Spirit of God raised that body from the dead. As I read the story, there is no incongruity when I pass from the story of His marvelous birth into the story of His incomparable ministry. He could raise the dead and open the eyes of the blind with the touch of His hand, speak words that no man ever heard before, and finally He Himself was raised from the dead. It is all one story, and it fits together like a beautiful and perfect mosaic.

The Intervention of God in Human History

Not only is the fashioning of the body of Christ the work of the Holy Spirit, but the Incarnation also represents an intervention of God in human history. From time to time and from the beginning to the consummation of the age, God miraculously and marvelously intervenes in the life of mankind.

The Spirit of God brooded over the face of the chaotic world and brought light out of darkness, form out of chaos, life out of death, and glory out of gloom and despair. That is the intervention of God in human history.

In the days of universal wickedness, Noah found grace in the sight of the Lord, and God intervened and spared Noah when He judged the world. In the days of universal idolatry, God called out Abraham to begin a new people and establish a new nation. In the days of universal apostasy, God raised up Elijah to be the champion of Jehovah. In the days of the beginning of a new dispensation of grace, God raised up John the Baptist to announce the coming of the great messianic king.

There is one other great intervention of God for which we wait. At the denouement of the age, at the consummation of time, Jesus will come to this earth visibly, gloriously, personally, bodily. And *every eye* shall *see* Him as He descends on the clouds of the *shekinah* glory of God.

God also intervened in human history when He came down and became one of us. Numbered with us, living our life, crying our tears, knowing our sorrows, bearing our sicknesses, dying our deaths, He was one of us. And we have the glorious promise of our resurrection through Him someday. This is the intervention of God in human history.

The Creation of a Body for Sacrifice

What is this marvelous thing that we call the Virgin Birth? It is the acceptance on the part of God almighty of a body to be offered in sacrifice for our sins. I spent six months preaching morning and evening on one chapter in the Book of Hebrews. If we had days and months, I would like to expound again the tenth chapter of the Book of Hebrews. There the author avows that the blood of bulls and goats could never wash our sins away. He points to the fact that those sacrifices that were offered again and again remind us of our yet future unforgiven iniquities. Such sacrifices in themselves do not avail. They are not sufficient to wash the stain of transgression out of our souls. Therefore, they are repeated again and again.

At the beginning of the age, up in heaven, a volunteer offered to give His life for our iniquities that we might be saved from the judgment of our sins. Hebrews 10 says that a body was prepared in order that God might make an atoning sacrifice for our transgressions. A spirit could never do that. That body, which was necessary to make propitiation for our sins, was framed by the Holy Spirit of God in the womb of the Virgin Mary, and God lived in that body. He was incarnate in the framing of that physical shape and form like a man, and He died once for all on the tree. There is no more an offering for sin. He came to make a sacrifice for our sins once for all, and in Him we have redemption, expiation, propitiation, forgiveness, cleansing, and all that God has in store for those who are washed clean and white in the blood of the Lamb. That is the gospel and that is the essence of the Virgin Birth—a body prepared for God in which He made sacrifice and atonement for our sins.

The Two Great Biological Miracles of God

There are two great biological miracles from the hand of almighty God. The first is seen in the creation of the first Adam with the miracle of mitosis or cell division. In every human body there are billions and trillions of human cells, and each of those cells has in it forty-six chromosomes, little threads to which are attached the genetic genes of heredity and life. God made Adam a biological miracle. In the generations that have followed, the miracle of mitosis or cell division occurs. Each cell has forty-six chromosomes, each chromosome splitting right down the middle, forty-six on one side and forty-six on the other side and the cellular wall dividing the middle. And so the body grows. However, in the female ovum God puts twenty-three chromosomes and in the male spermatozoon He puts twenty-three chromosomes; and when they come together in conception, there are forty-six again. That is the first great biological miracle of God—the miracle of mitosis or cell division, conception, the creation of human life.

The government has been having Senate hearings to determine when human life begins. The answer to that is as plain as $1 + 1 = 2$ or $2 + 2 = 4$. Life begins when twenty-three chromosomes of the female ovum and twenty-three chromosomes of the male spermatozoon come together. You cannot escape it. You cannot deny it. That is the miracle of life.

The second great biological miracle of God is this: The Lord's hand reached down and entered into that genetic change of mitosis and did a creative work unparalleled in the history of mankind. Without the spermatozoon He created a body for Christ in which God incarnated Himself to make atonement for our sins and to be our Lord and brother and friend and fellow pilgrim and sympathetic High Priest and Savior and King forever and ever. When I try to say it, it is such a vast, incomparable, and heavenly truth that I want to apologize to the Lord for saying it so poorly and so stammeringly! But having seen it and read about it and observed all that Jesus means in this world, then I understand what I read on the pages of the Bible. This Virgin Birth, this incarnation of God, becomes so beautifully clear.

It starts in Genesis 3:15, where it says that the seed of the woman would crush Satan's head. A woman does not have seed. A man has seed. From the beginning aged rabbis would pour over that passage. They would never know what it meant until the story was fulfilled in the birth of our Lord. The seed of the woman—Jesus, God Incarnate—would bruise Satan's head. That is what it meant, and we did not know it until thousands of years later.

The incomparable prophecy of Isaiah declared:

> Behold, a virgin shall conceive, and bear a son, and shall call his name Immanuel (which being interpreted is God is with us) (Is. 7:14).

God incarnate—that is what it meant.

The beautiful prophecy in Isaiah 9 says:

> For unto us a child is born, unto us a son is given: and the government shall be upon his shoulder; and his name shall be called Wonderful, Counselor, The mighty God, The everlasting Father, The Prince of Peace (Is. 9:6).

That is what it meant, God incarnate.

This incomparable prelude of praise begins the Gospel of John:

> In the beginning was the Word, and the Word was with God, and the Word was God. And the Word was made flesh, and dwelt among us, (and we beheld his glory, the glory as of the only begotten of the Father,) full of grace and truth (John 1:1, 14).

That is what it meant: The Word that was made flesh is God incarnate.

The magnificent passage of the apostle Paul in Galatians avows:

> But when the fullness of the time was come, God sent forth his Son, made of a woman, made under the law [Man did not have anything to do with it],
> To redeem them that were under the law, that we might receive the adoption of sons (Gal. 4:4–5).

We become brothers and sisters of Jesus in the family of God through our brother, Christ Jesus.

That is what it meant in that marvelous last invitation in Revelation:

> I Jesus have sent mine angel to testify unto you these things in the churches. I am the root and the offspring of David, and the bright and morning star. [How could it be? He is the root of David. He was before David. He is a predecessor. Before David was I am. I am the root and the offspring of David. Through His mother Mary He was of the house and lineage of David. I understand it now.]
>
> And the Spirit and the bride say, Come. And let him that heareth say, Come. And let him that is athirst come. And whosoever will, let him take the water of life freely.
>
> He which testifieth these things saith, Surely, I come quickly. [A human, bodily Jesus Christ, our Savior, God Incarnate in the flesh. Oh, that all of us might pray the responding, answering prayer of the sainted apostle John] Amen. Even so, come, Lord Jesus (Rev. 22:16, 17, 20.)

What a glorious word! What a marvelous gospel! What a precious hope! Waiting, watching, praying, serving, until that same virgin-born Lord Jesus comes again!

9

Is the Man Jesus Also God?

Let us look at Matthew's account of the crucifixion of Jesus.

And they that passed by reviled him, wagging their heads,

And saying, Thou that destroyest the temple, and buildest it in three days, save thyself. If thou be the Son of God, come down from the cross.

Likewise also the chief priests mocking him, with the scribes and elders, said,

He saved others; himself he cannot save. If he be the King of Israel, let him now come down from the cross, and we will believe him.

He trusted in God; let him deliver him now, if he will have him: for he said, I am the Son of God (Matt. 27:39–43).

Jesus said, "I am the Son of God." He said, "He that hath seen me hath seen the Father." He said, "Before Abraham was, I am." He said, "The great, Almighty, omnipotent I am."

If someone pointed out a man to you and said: "That fellow over there says that he is God," what would you think? You would almost instinctively react: "Really? He is God? He must be a nut! He must be insane!"

Let us consider three possibilities as we face such an incredulous and incredible claim. (1) Jesus said He was God, but He knew He was not. Therefore, He is a charlatan, a purposive, acknowledged deceiver. He is a stated liar. (2) Jesus said He was God, but He was self-deceived. He was insane, abnormal, and mentally disordered. (3) He never said He was God. The disciples placed those words in His mouth, and they are the charlatans and the deceivers.

Jesus—a Liar?

Let us look at that first possibility for a moment: Jesus said He was God, though He knew He was not God. He was a purposive deceiver, a charlatan, a liar. Even the most fanatical and bitter enemies of the Lord, unbelievers, have rarely pressed this conclusion. The reason for it is apparent. We have in the Bible page after page of what Jesus taught, and nowhere does it sound like the teachings of a liar or a deceiver.

This passage was copied out of one of the great histories of the world. It was written by William H. Lecky, an Irish historian of the last century. Lecky was certainly no friend to revealed religion, but he wrote this in his great book *History of European Morals:*

> The character of Jesus has not only been the highest pattern of virtue, but the strongest incentive to its practice, and has exerted so deep an influence, that it may be truly said, that the simple record of three short years of his active life has done more to regenerate and to soften mankind, than all the disquisitions of philosophers and than all the exhortations of moralists.

It would be hard to conclude that the incomparable, ethical, moral spiritual teachings of Jesus were based upon a lie.

It is difficult to persuade oneself that the beautiful, perfect, sinless, noble, virtuous character of our Lord is that of an imposter and deceiver.

The late C. S. Lewis, the brilliant journalist of England who was marvelously converted, wrote these words in the book, *The Case for Christianity:*

> I am trying to prevent anyone from saying the really silly thing that people often say about Jesus: "I'm ready to accept Jesus as a great moral teacher, but I do not accept His claim to be God!" That's the one thing we must not say. A man who was merely a man and said the sort of things Jesus said would not be a great moral teacher. He'd either be a lunatic on a level with a man who says he's a poached egg, or else He'd be the Devil of Hell. You must make your choice. Either this man was and is the Son of God, or else a madman or something worse. You can shut Him up for a fool, you can spit at Him and kill Him for a demon, or you can fall at His feet and call Him Lord and God. But don't let us come with any patronizing nonsense about His being a great human teacher. He hasn't left that open to us.

Is the Man Jesus Also God?

It is unthinkable and unimaginable that the beautiful, holy, noble life of our Lord is that of an imposter, a charlatan, and a deceiver.

JESUS—A LUNATIC?

The second possibility is that though Jesus said He was God, He was actually mentally aberrated. He was self-deceived. This would provoke on our part a discussion of Jesus as a psychotic, a paranoid, or a megalomaniac with illusions of grandeur.

He is God? Well, we have His life spread here before us in minutest detail. We have His words, page after page of them. Read them. When you read those profound words of the Lord Jesus, do they sound to you like the words of a man who is mentally disordered, psychotic, or paranoid? I have here something I copied from a great psychiatrist named J. T. Fisher.

> If you were to take the sum total of all authoritative articles ever written by the most gifted and qualified of psychologists and psychiatrists on the subject of mental hygiene—if you were to combine them and refine them and cleave out the excess verbage—and if you were to have these unadulterated bits of pure scientific knowledge concisely expressed by the most capable of living poets, you would have an awkward and incomplete summation of the "Sermon on the Mount," and it would suffer immeasureably through comparison. For nearly two thousand years the Christian world has been holding in its hand the complete answer to its restless and fruitless yearnings. Here rests [in the words of the Lord Jesus in the Sermon on the Mount] the blueprint for successful human life with optimum mental health and contentment.

When you read the words of the Lord Jesus, does it sound to you as though they are the words of a man who is a lunatic? They certainly do not to me. And they do not to you or any right-thinking person. Never a man spake like that man!

The first possibility: He said He was God, but He knew He was not. He was a deceiver and an imposter. The second possibility: He said He was God, but He was self-deceived, mentally aberrated, insane.

JESUS—DEIFIED BY HIS DISCIPLES?

Now the third possibility: He never said He was God. Rather, the disciples put those words in His mouth. They deified Him. Well, let us honestly look at the possibility of the deification of the Lord by His disciples.

(1) No one has ever lived who was a poorer candidate for deification than Jesus. I can well imagine the Greeks deifying Alexander the Great, the originator of the great Hellenistic empire. I can understand how the Romans deified Augustus Caesar. He had the entire civilized world in his iron hand, and I can understand how they bowed down before him. But not in ten thousand lifetimes could I ever understand how the monotheistic Jews could deify a poor carpenter from Nazareth who was crucified as a felon! It just does not make sense. He was the poorest candidate for deification imaginable.

(2) In every cardinal point concerning what the Messiah was like, Jesus' conception of Himself was diametrically opposite to the conception of all the Jewish people, including the disciples. Without exception, the Jewish nation, including the disciples, looked upon the Messiah as One who would bring in the messianic kingdom and who would lead an army victoriously against the Roman slavemasters—the men who had mistreated them, insulted them, and ground them to powder! You cannot imagine the hatred of the Jew (who possessed the oracles of God) toward the pagan Roman who had crushed him. A few years after the life of our Lord, in A.D. 66, the Jews mounted that awesome revolt against Rome that ended in the destruction of their nation in A.D. 70. Without exception, the disciples and the Jewish nation were looking for a Messiah to lead them to heights of splendor—a materialistic kingdom that was filled with grandeur and glory! But the Lord Jesus said, "My kingdom is not of this world." His idea of a suffering Messiah was unthinkable to them.

(3) The disciples were ethically, religiously, morally, and psychologically incapable of performing such a miracle of deification. It was they who had to be convinced. Simon Peter before a little maid said: "I do not even know Him. I have never heard of Him." John took Mary, the mother of Jesus, to his home to care for her the rest of her life. To John it was over. Every dream had been crushed to the dust of the ground. The gifted Saul of Tarsus, who became Paul the apostle, said, "I am the least of the saints because I persecuted the church of God. When those who believed in Christ were put to death, I cast my vote against them." The men who most of all had to be convinced of our Lord were the preachers themselves. They could not have invented the life of our Lord. Nor is any man capable of it. They

could not have manufactured the story of the Resurrection and deity of Jesus, knowing it was a lie. Much less could they have laid down their lives for the deception. Psychologically it is impossible.

JESUS—THE LORD!

Then there must be another possibility. What was it that changed those followers of the Lord, shattered and broken, into flaming evangelists who converted the Roman empire and did away with all of the gods of the Greeks and Romans? At that time the whole world bowed before idols. Today I do not know anyone anywhere in the world who bows before those Roman gods. What happened that transformed those men from broken, shattered, defeated followers into flaming martyrs for Christ? It must be the fourth possibility: Jesus is who He said He was—the Son of God.

That is the witness of the primary documents. When you go back to the beginning, this is the universal testimony of the prophets and of the apostles, Jesus is God! The prophets said:

> Behold, a virgin shall conceive, and bear a son, and shall call his name Immanuel [God with us] (Is. 7:14).

> For unto us a child is born, unto us a son is given: and the government shall be upon his shoulder; and his name shall be called Wonderful, Counselor, The mighty God, The everlasting Father, The Prince of Peace (Is. 9:6).

Going back to the primary documents, we read from John the apostle:

> In the beginning was the Word [*Logos*], and the Word was with God, and the Word was God. And the Word was made flesh, and dwelt among us, (and we beheld his glory, the glory as of the only begotten of the Father,) full of grace and truth (John 1:1, 14).

Again we look to the words of the primary documents. Paul wrote:

> [Jesus] is the image of the invisible God, the firstborn of every creature:
> For by him were all things created, that are in heaven, and that are in earth, visible and invisible, whether they be thrones, or dominions, or principalities, or powers: all things were created by him, and for him:
> And he is before all things, and by him all things consist (Col. 1:15–17).

91

For in him dwelleth all the fullness of the Godhead bodily (Col. 2:9).

Looking for that blessed hope, and the glorious appearing of the great God and our Savior Jesus Christ (Titus 2:13).

From the beginning of that first Christian century, Jesus was worshiped as God. It is strange to me to find in my study of Christian history that the heresy first faced by the church was Docetic Gnosticism. "Docetic" comes from the Greek word *dokeō,* which means "to seem" or "to appear." "Gnostic" is a reference to someone who is proud of his superior knowledge. *Gnōsis* is the Greek word for knowledge. So Docetic Gnostics were men who proclaimed themselves to have superior wisdom and knowledge. They said that Jesus just appeared to have a body. He just appeared to be human, but actually He was God. So deep and profound and fundamentally dynamic was the impression of Jesus as being God that the first heresy was that He was not man at all. He just appeared to have a body. The worship of Jesus as God in those beginning Christian centuries was the unique, dynamic characteristic of the Christian faith.

In A.D. 112 Pliny the Younger, the Roman governor of the Roman province of Bithynia, wrote a letter to Trajan, the Caesar, the Roman emperor. The occasion for the letter was that the temples of Bithynia were being emptied. Nobody was worshiping the Greek gods or the Roman gods—Jupiter, Mercury, or any of the rest. The temples were empty, and Pliny was writing to Trajan about what to do. In the letter Pliny explained why the Greek temples were empty. He said: "The Christians have swept the province of Bithynia. They gather on the first day of the week to sing hymns to Jesus as God." The beginning of the Christian faith was this: Jesus is God!

There are four points I want to share with you concerning Jesus, the man who is God.

WHAT HE SAID ONLY GOD COULD SAY

Look at the words Jesus said. If anyone else ever said those words, he would be blaspheming, but on the lips of Jesus the words seem apropos. What Jesus said about Himself, only God could say: I am the light; I am the way; I am the truth; I am the vine; I am the life; Ask in My name; I will rise from the dead; Whoso eateth My flesh and drinketh My blood hath eternal life

92

and I will raise him up in the last day; Keep my commandments; I am the Resurrection; I am from above; I am the light of the world; I am come down from heaven; Before Abraham was, I am; All power is given unto Me in heaven and in earth; I am greater than the temple; A greater than Solomon is here; I am the Lord of the Sabbath; He that hath seen Me hath seen the Father; Come unto Me, all ye that labor and are heavy laden, and I will give you rest; You call me Master and Lord, and ye say well, for so I am; Heaven and earth shall pass away, but My words shall not pass away; Hereafter ye shall see the Son of man sitting on the right hand of power and coming in the clouds of heaven; This is My blood of the new covenant which is shed for many for the remission of sin; Lo, I am with you alway, even unto the end of the world; The Son of man shall come and then shall He reward every man according to his works. Those are the words of God, and they are blasphemous if they are not from the lips of Him who is the great I AM.

THE LIFE THAT HE LIVED IS THE LIFE OF GOD

What He was in Himself, the life that He lived, is the life of God. What He was is what God is. Jesus—holy, sinless, pure, without fault—was the perfect man, and only God is perfect.

Think through the great men of the earth. Let us ask of them personal perfection. Moses, are you the sinless, ideal man? Moses replies: "After taking care of the people for forty years, I was interdicted from entering the Promised Land and died in the plains of Moab because in my vile anger I slew a man on one occasion and on another I struck the rock instead of speaking to it as God had commanded. It is not I."

David was the man after God's own heart and I come to David and say, "Are you the ideal, sinless man?" David replies, "When I had it in my heart to build the temple, God said, 'No, you are a man of blood and war.'"

Jesus said that John the Baptist was the greatest man born of women. I approach John the Baptist and ask him, "Are you the sinless and ideal man?" He replies: "I am from beneath, He is from heaven. I am not worthy to loosen the latchet of His shoes."

I approach the apostle Paul and ask him, "Are you the ideal man?" Paul replies, "I am the least of his servants because I persecuted the church of God."

Where shall I find that ideal life? It is impossible for mankind to create it. He cannot do it. Even the fiction writers throughout history have not been able to create the ideal life.

Read of Achilles in Homer's *Iliad* or Odysseus in his *Odyssey*. Is it Achilles? Is it Odysseus? Homer could not create the perfect man. Virgil's Aeneas in his *Aeneid*—Is it Aeneas? Virgil could not create him. The Agamemnon of Aeschylus—Could Aeschylus create him? No—and on and on. No man could create the holy, heavenly life of the Lord Jesus.

Even the enemies of our Lord, such as Pilate, said, "I find no fault in Him at all." Judas said, "I have betrayed innocent blood." Pilate's wife said to her husband, "Have thou nothing to do with that just man." One of the malefactors crucified with Him said, "This man hath done nothing amiss." The centurion who presided over His execution said, "Truly this man is the Son of God."

Our Lord is unique, apart. There is none like Him. To the artist He is the One altogether lovely. To the architect He is the chief cornerstone. To the astronomer He is the sun of righteousness. To the baker He is the living bread. To the banker He is the riches of the world. To the biologist He is the life of life. To the builder He is the sure foundation. To the doctor He is the great physician. To the educator He is the master teacher. To the engineer He is the true and living way. To the farmer He is the sower and the Lord of the harvest. To the florist He is the rose of Sharon and the lily of the valley. To the geologist He is the rock of ages. To the horticulturist He is the true vine. To the judge He is the righteous judge of all men. To the juror He is the faithful and true witness. To the lawyer He is a great counselor and advocate. To the newspaper man He is the good tidings of great joy. To the philanthropist He is the unspeakable gift. To the philosopher He is the wisdom of God. To the preacher He is the Word of God. To the sculptor He is the living stone. To the servant He is the good master. To the statesman He is the desire of all nations. To the student He is the incarnate truth. To the theologian He is the author and finisher of our faith. To the toiler He is the giver of rest. To the sinner He is the Lamb of God that taketh away the sin of the world. To the Christian He is our Lord and our God. There is none like Him. Nor is it possible for human genius to create Him. He is unique and apart. He is our Lord God.

Is the Man Jesus Also God?

What Jesus Did Only God Could Do

Not only were the words that He spoke the words of God. Not only was the life that He lived the life of God. What Jesus did only God could do. He could speak to the raging wind and waves, "Be still," and they were quiet at His feet. He would say to a paralytic, "Stand up," and he who had never walked stood up. He would say to the leper, "Be thou clean," and the leper was whole again. He could say to the dead, "Come forth," and the dead lived again.

Jesus said, "The third day I shall rise from the dead." Romans 1:4 has in it the marvelous Greek word *horizō,* from which our English word "horizon" comes. The horizon is the demarcation that lies between the earth and the sky. That word, *horizō,* is translated "declared." Jesus is "declared," "pointed out," "marked out" to be the Son of God with power, according to the spirit of holiness, by the resurrection from the dead.

There is an amusing incident out of the life of Napoleon Bonaparte. A man came up to him and said that he was starting a new religion but that he was having trouble getting people to believe in him. Napoleon flippantly remarked: "Why that should be easy. Just get yourself crucified and the third day rise from the dead. Then they will believe in you." What Jesus did only God can do.

His Promise Is the Promise of God

The hope and the promise that He offers is the hope and the promise of God. In life He is our friend, fellow pilgrim, and companion. Down any lonely road He will walk with us. Facing any confrontation He is there to help us. In any sorrow He is strength and comfort. In life He is our great friend. The hope and the promise we have in Christ is that of God.

In our church there was a godly family with a little girl in our Sunday school. The little girl contracted meningitis and the doctors said that the child would soon die. As the mother held the little girl in her arms, the child began to go blind. She cried to her mother, "Mother, Mother, it is getting dark, and I am afraid!" The mother comforted the child with this word: "Sweet, precious child, Jesus is with us in the dark, just as He is with us in the light. Don't be afraid." The comfort of Jesus is the comfort of God.

Walking through Baylor Hospital some months ago I met

95

one of our young women. I did not know she was there. She was facing tests. After the tests were run, the doctors said to her: "You have the Lou Gehrig nerve disease and it is terminal. There is no cure and there is no hope, and you will soon die." Later she said to me, "I want you to pray with me and talk to me."

What would you have said? What did I say? I said: "Dear young lady, it is God, it is Jesus who opens that door into the other world, not the doctor, not the hospital, not the surgeon. It is Jesus." I told her, "I may go through that door before you do. I may see His face before you do. It is in God's hands. All of us face that inevitable hour. It is not a matter of whether or not. It is just a matter of when. Is it today? Is it tomorrow? Is it the next day? It does not matter. When that door is opened into heaven, it will be His nail-pierced hands that are extended to us. And when we are welcomed into glory, it will be the loving face of our Lord that we see. Do not be afraid."

> The golden sun, the silvery moon,
>   And all the stars that shine,
> Were made by His omnipotent hand,
>   And He's a friend of mine.
>
> When He shall come with trumpet sound
>   To head the conquering line,
> The whole world will bow before His feet,
>   And He's a friend of mine.

Do not be afraid. Our God is the Lord Jesus and He is our best and closest friend, our Savior forever.

10

The Unchanging Christ

The author of Hebrews is writing to a congregation of Hebrew Christians somewhere in the Roman world. He says:

> Remember them which have the rule over you, who have spoken unto you the word of God: whose faith follow, considering the end of their conversation [the end of their life].
>
> Jesus Christ the same yesterday, and today, and for ever (Heb. 13:7–8).

Reading those two verses you might wonder what connection they have. They seem so diversely opposite. But no. The tremendous text, "Jesus Christ the same yesterday, and today, and for ever," arises out of a sorrow in the heart of the little congregation to whom this author is addressing an epistle of comfort and exhortation.

Evidently the pastors whom they first knew had died. The tenses of the verb are in the past. The writer is encouraging them, despite their sorrow of heart, to look at the beautiful life of faith exhibited and lived before them by their shepherds. He is exhorting the little congregation to follow the faithful example of their pastors, remembering them with gratitude and thanksgiving to God. He then points them away from the dying and fading ministry of an earthly shepherd to the ministry in Christ Jesus that shall abide forever.

The pastor may die. His work may be finished. His last sermon may be on the study desk. The final benediction may be ready to pronounce, but Jesus Christ our Lord abides forever.

What He Was He Is and Ever Shall Be

Our Lord is the same now as He was and as He ever shall be. What He was, He is; and what He is, He will be forever. He is presented to us in the Holy Scriptures as the great omnipotent Creator in the untold ages of the past.

> All things were made by him; and without him was not any thing made that was made (John 1:3).

> For by him were all things created, that are in heaven, and that are in earth, visible and invisible, whether they be thrones, or dominions, or principalities, or powers: all things were created by him, and for him (Col. 1:16).

The mighty creator of the universe and of all that we see is Jesus our Lord, the Christ of yesterday.

But the Christ of today is no different. He is still that same omnipotent creator. We live and we stand in the midst of omnipotent miracles. Every harvest is a gift of His creative hand, a banquet of manna spread before us in the wilderness. On a thousand hills He is still performing the miracle of turning water into the fruit of the vine. Even these marvelously beautiful flowers are made by Him out of the muck and the mire of the ground—a miracle of beauty. The unchanging Christ—as He was yesterday, so He is today and ever shall be.

At the consummation of the age in the glorious tomorrow He says, "Behold, I make all things new" (Rev. 21:5a). John describes the work of His omnipotent hands in Revelation with these words,

> And I saw a new heaven and a new earth: for the first heaven and the first earth were passed away (Rev. 21:1).

He is the same yesterday, the same today, and the same forever.

He is thus no different in His atoning grace. Before the foundation of the world was laid, He was the Lamb of sacrifice. Somewhere in the dim ages of the past, according to Hebrews 10, He volunteered to be a propitiation, a vicarious sacrifice, for our sin. All of the sacrifices of the Old Covenant pointed in type to Him who is the Savior of the world. That is our Christ of yesterday.

He is no less abounding in atoning grace today—this same Lord Jesus. Every grain of wheat that falls in the ground and dies that others might live is a picture of our Lord's atoning mercy in our hearts today. He speaks to us in forgiveness, and He delivers us from the bondage and the judgment of sin. He is also our personal atoning sacrifice. What He was before the foundation of the world and what He is in our human experience today, He also is forever.

He is the Song of Songs. The song of the ages is the song of the redeemed family of God in the beautiful heaven to come. Remember it? "Worthy is the Lamb that was slain to receive power, and riches, and wisdom, and strength, and honour, and glory, and blessing. [For He hath] redeemed us to God by [His] blood out of every kindred, and tongue and people, and nation; and hast made us unto our God kings and priests: and we shall reign on the earth" (Lev. 5:12, 9–10). He is the same Lord in atoning grace yesterday and today and forever.

He is the unchanging Christ in His shepherdly care. The story of our Lord in the Old Covenant is the story of a seeking, loving heart. After the fall in the Garden of Eden He sought our first parents. He called Moses to deliver His people out of the slavery and bondage of Egypt. Isaiah presents a beautiful picture of our Lord:

> He shall feed his flock like a shepherd: he shall gather the lambs with his arm, and carry them in his bosom, and shall gently lead those that are with young (Is. 40:11).

The picture of our Christ in the ages past is one of shepherdly and loving care.

He is no less and no different our loving Lord today. He speaks to us words of help, encouragement, and comfort. He stands by our side in time of need. He has promised saying, "I will never leave thee nor forsake thee." Every dawning of a new day and the rising of the sun is the shining of His dear face, promising blessing for the needs of the day.

What He was yesterday, He is today—our great physician, deliverer, healer, helper, and comforter. What He is today, He is forever and ever. He has only gone in order that He might prepare a way and a place for us. Someday He will come for His own. Every sunset is a reminder that Jesus is opening a door for us into heaven. Christ—the unchanging Lord—is the same yesterday and today and forever.

A Denial in the Text

The beautiful avowal in the text has in it a denial and an affirmation. What is denied is that in Christ there is ever change, either by circumstance, time, history, mood, or provocation.

No, our Lord never changes. We change. One day we are strong, and the next day we are weak. One day we are filled with firm resolve, and the next day we are weak as water. One day we seem to be in a moment of holiness and dedication, and the next day we are as unstable as the wind. We change, but He never changes. In Him is no variableness or shadow cast by turning. He is the same yesterday, today, and forever.

Time changes us. Like an autumnal leaf on which the frost has fallen, we age and finally are buried in the ground. Our days are few and fleeting. Each one of us can see the end of the way. But for Him there is nothing but a present forever and forever. He is ever the same—His preincarnate existence, His incarnation, and His glorious resurrected, immortalized life.

Moods change us. We are one way today, and the next day we are another way. One day we are like a rock, and another day we are like a reed. But His heart never changes. He is ever the same—our great, glorious, loving, compassionate Savior.

Circumstances change us. The butler who was liberated from prison and exalted in Pharaoh's household forgot the lad Joseph who was languishing in the dungeon. So often do circumstances change us. If we are exalted or made famous or affluent or successful, it is so easy to forget those who are poor, degraded, lost, or submerged. But our Lord never changes. He is the same loving, compassionate Lord toward the poor, the forgotten, the lost, the unkempt, the dirty, and the outcast as He is to those who are kingly in life and successful in experience. Circumstances change us, but He never changes.

The Affirmation in the Text

Not only is there a denial in the text, but there is also a tremendous affirmation. The affirmation concerns the immutability of our Lord, the unchangingness of our Christ. He is the same throughout all the ages of the ages, the eternal Christ. His name in the Old Covenant is Jehovah. His name in the New Covenant is "Jehovah our Salvation," the root meaning of His personal name, Jesus. Whether He is known as "Jehovah" in the Old Covenant or "Jehovah our Salvation," i.e., Jesus, in the New Covenant, He is always the same.

Before He was born, the angel announced that His name would be called "Jesus" because He would save His people from their sins. When He was born, He was given the name Jesus, "Jehovah our Salvation."

As a child, He was holy. We read in Acts 4 of the apostles praying in the name of "thy holy child Jesus" (Acts 4:27). A needy soul cried, "Jesus, thou Son of David, have mercy upon me!" When He was crucified, He was crucified with that name. The inscription above His cross was, "This is Jesus of Nazareth, the King of the Jews." When He was raised from the dead, He was that same Lord Jesus, "Jehovah our Salvation." When Jesus stood in the midst of His disciples, glorified and immortalized, He was that same Lord Jesus. When Saul, on the way to Damascus to persecute Christians, fell blinded at His feet, he cried, "Who art thou, Lord?" And the Lord replied, "I am Jesus whom thou persecutest." In His glorified, immortalized life, He is still the same Lord Jesus. In the concluding, apocalyptic book of the Bible we read,

> I Jesus have sent mine angel to testify unto you these things in the churches. I am the root and the offspring of David, and the bright and morning star (Rev. 22:16).

When the final consummation of the world is brought to pass, who will be descending in clouds of glory from heaven?

> This same Jesus, which is taken up from you into heaven, shall so come in like manner as ye have seen him go into heaven (Acts 1:11b).

It is Jesus for whom we are looking. The same face, the same tender voice, the same loving heart—He never changes! The benediction in the Apocalypse closes thus,

> He which testifieth these things, saith, Surely I come quickly. Amen. Even so, come, Lord Jesus (Rev. 22:20).

If we know our hearts, we are ready. Come, come, Lord Jesus. He is the same unchanging person yesterday, today, and forever.

He is also unchanging in His offices. His name by title is "Messiah" (Hebrew) or "Christ" (Greek). The Jew with his Messiah, the Greek with his Christ—all the gentile world of every nation find themselves one in Him. He is the Anointed One, the Christ, the Messiah.

He is anointed for His prophetic office. As Kings 19 describes the anointing of Elisha for the office of a prophet, so Christ Jesus was anointed for the office of prophet. Thus does Simon Peter speak in Acts 10, "God anointed Jesus of Nazareth with the Holy Ghost and with power" (v. 38). He is the anointed prophet. His message is authoritative forever. He is our tremendous representative from God to teach us the way of everlasting life. He is our great anointed prophet and teacher.

He is our anointed priest. All the priests of the Old Covenant were anointed, but they faced a terminal day of their ministries before God and men. Aaron, anointed of God to be the high priest, died on Mt. Hor. All of his successors died. The ashes of the shepherd were mingled with the ashes of the flock. But He, our great High Priest, is anointed forever after the order of Melchizedek. He has an enduring priesthood that never dies. Forever and ever He is our intercessor and our mediator before the throne of grace in heaven, anointed of God to be our representative, our unchanging High Priest.

He is anointed of God to be King over heaven and earth and over the things beneath the earth. As we read in Psalm 45, "God, thy God, hath anointed thee with the oil of gladness above thy fellows" (v. 7), to be King over all the earth. He is the Head of the church. He is the King of the hosts of heaven, and He is the Lord of all creation. To Him give all the prophets witness.

> Wherefore God also hath highly exalted him, and given him a name which is above every name:
> That at the name of Jesus every knee shall bow, of things in heaven, and things in earth, and things under the earth;
> And that every tongue should confess that Jesus Christ is Lord, to the glory of God the Father (Phil. 2:9–11).

The great affirmation is this: He is the same yesterday, today, and forever in His enduring offices.

The great affirmation applies to His presence. As He was yesterday and as He shall be tomorrow, so is our Lord Jesus to us now. He is our friend and our companion. He walks by our side, and He ministers to our daily needs. He breaks for us the Bread of Life as He did for the five thousand in the days of His flesh. He rides with us in the boat on the storm-tossed seas of life. He shows us the right side of the boat on which to cast our nets. He walks with us to Emmaus as He did in the days long ago. He opens to us the Scriptures as He did to the two disciples. He rebukes us when selfishly we seek our own personal advancement. He washes our feet at the close of the day when we are soiled with the pilgrim journey. He comes to us over the stormy waves when we begin to sink. When we are weary, He calls to us to rest in Him.

The unchanging Christ lives today. Above every lake is His abiding presence; above every storm is His mighty and omnipotent voice; every meal finds Him with His face uplifted in blessing and thanksgiving. Our Lord is the great Unchanging One. By the side of every open grave, He stands and weeps, touched with the feeling of our infirmities. When the burden is too heavy for us to bear, His shoulders share with us the heavy weight. The great Unchanging Christ: as He was yesterday, as He will be tomorrow, so is He thus to us now.

The immutable, unchanging Christ is the Lord of an expanding kingdom given to Him in promise by the Father. Because He condescended to die, God also highly exalted Him and gave Him a people. I do not know a finer definition of election than that. Because Christ bowed His heart in sorrow for our sins and poured out His life in vicarious suffering that we might be forgiven, God has promised Him a people and an expanding and an enduring kingdom. And it grows and grows until it covers all heaven and earth.

When our Lord ascended to the top of the Mount of Olives, He looked down upon that little band who worshiped at His feet. Then He rose higher and the vision expanded: before Him was spread out the city of Jerusalem. He rose higher and the vision expanded: before Him was all of the Holy Land, Samaria, and Galilee. He rose higher and the vision expanded: before Him was spread the whole expanse of the earth. Thus is the kingdom of our Lord.

He walked by the shores of the little Sea of Galilee, and He called Peter and James and John and other followers who forsook all and followed Him. History passes, the vision expands, time multiplies, and an unseen Presence is walking by the shores of the greater sea, the Mediterranean. And He calls and there are those who forsake all and follow Him. And the days pass and time passes and history moves on. And the Lord is walking by a still greater sea, the vast Atlantic. And He calls men and women who forsake all and follow Him. And the days march on, and the Lord walks by the shores of all of the continents of the earth and we hear His voice, and there are those by the thousands and by the millions who forsake all to follow Him. The kingdom of this world has become the kingdom of our Lord, the unchanging Christ, and He shall reign forever and ever.

> All hail the pow'r of Jesus' name!
> Let angels prostrate fall;
> Bring forth the royal diadem,
> And crown Him Lord of all;
>
> Ye chosen seed of Israel's race,
> Ye ransomed from the fall,
> Hail Him who saves you by His grace,
> And crown Him Lord of all.

Thus His great promise in salvation is ever the same. It never changes. That glorious good news heard in the first century is the same glorious good news of the gospel that is repeated on a thousand tongues on a thousand lips today—the same unchanging appeal. The gospel message that saved Saul of Tarsus on the road to Damascus is the same wonderful gospel message that saves us today. It never changes.

He is the same Lord who seeks us and loves us. He is the same Christ, the Lamb of God who poured out His life for us. The same abounding mercy that reaches and touches our souls and our hearts and the same omnipotent promise of eternal and everlasting life is the same today as it was in the first century. It never changes. What a wonderful word and what a glorious promise of our Lord! If I will look to Him, if I will open my heart to Him, if I will receive Him in all of His grace and love and mercy, I will be saved forever and ever.

> How firm a foundation, ye saints of the Lord,
> Is laid for your faith in His excellent Word!
> What more can He say than to you He hath said—
> To you, who for refuge to Jesus have fled?
>
> The soul that on Jesus hath leaned for repose,
> I will not, I will not desert to his foes;
> That soul, though all hell should endeavor to shake,
> I'll never—no, never—no, never forsake!

The Unchanging Christ

The unchanging Christ with His unchanging gospel and the unchanging promise and hope of a salvation that endures forever! Thus God has wrought for us a mercy and a grace that touches the human heart, that lifts up the fallen soul, that comforts the discouraged spirit, that delivers us from the oppressive judgment of sin in that great final day of the Lord and that will present us some day in His grace and in His goodness faultless and without spot or blemish in the presence of His great glory.

Oh, that I had a voice worthy to praise the Lamb! Oh, that I had a tongue that could expound the marvelous grace of God! Oh, that there were words with which I could extol the marvelous goodness and love and grace of our Lord!

Look and live! Believe and be saved! Wash and be clean! Follow Him, for His path leads us up the glory road, up the highway of holiness to the beautiful eternal city of God. Bless and praise His name forever! Yesterday, today, and forever, the unchanging Christ!

11

The Meaning for Us of the God-Man

> And they that passed by reviled him, wagging their heads,
>
> And saying, Thou that destroyest the temple, and buildest it in three days, save thyself. If thou be the Son of God, come down from the cross.
>
> Likewise also the chief priests mocking him, with the scribes and elders, said,
>
> He saved others; himself he cannot save. If he be the King of Israel, let him now come down from the cross, and we will believe him.
>
> He trusted in God; let him deliver him now, if he will have him: for he said, I am the Son of God (Matt. 27:39–43).

Note also the reaction of the centurion who supervised the crucifixion:

> Now when the centurion, and they that were with him, watching Jesus, saw the earthquake, and those things that were done, they feared greatly, saying, Truly this was the Son of God (Matt. 27:54).

How difficult is the conception that in one person living, moving, breathing, speaking, was God—God of very God and man of very man! How difficult is the conception that in one person could be found true deity and true humanity! This difficulty pressed with unbelieving force upon the minds of the Jewish people. How could the great, mighty, omnipotent Jehovah God, revealed amidst the thunder and lightning and earthquakes on Mt. Sinai in the giving of the law, ever be a mere man?

The room in which the worst sinners and traitors were judged, sentenced, and condemned was the very judgment hall in which the Jews saw Him judged and condemned. Their own leaders—the high priest and the priests of the temple, the learned Sadducees and Pharisees, and the doctors and scribes of the law—clamored for His blood and accused Him unto death. There on that hill just outside the city gates is the place where He was executed, crucified as a malefactor, as a criminal. His own surviving relatives lived among them. How could He be God?

No less so is the difficulty of that conception pressed upon the minds and judgments of His disciples and His own apostles. They were expecting a messianic kingdom of earthly splendor, and then they saw the promised Messiah—the symbol of their hope—crucified unto death and buried. Buried with Him in the dust and heart of the ground was every vision they had entertained for a triumphant messianic kingdom. We can hardly describe the abject disappointment, frustration, and despair of those apostles and disciples when they saw Jesus die. Even the apostle Thomas who was with the Lord through all the days of His flesh, who saw His wonderful miracles, who listened to His incomparable words, even Thomas said, "Except I . . . put my finger into the print of his nails, and thrust my hand into his side, I will not believe" (John 20:25).

One of the most unusual little addenda in the whole Bible to me is in Matthew 28:17. This is the description of five hundred of the disciples of our Lord that were meeting Him on an appointed mountain in Galilee.

> And when they saw him, they worshiped him: but some doubted.

They were looking at Him immortalized, glorified, and raised from the dead, "but some doubted." The difficulty of deity and humanity in one person was beyond what the human mind could contain.

But when the apostles and the disciples were persuaded and convinced of it, they laid down their lives for the truth of it. All of them were martyred except John, who was exiled to die of exposure and starvation. The announcement of the gospel that they proclaimed to the world literally changed the course of human civilization. That announcement (*kerugma*), that preaching of the gospel that Jesus is God, that He is the Lord of heaven and earth, that He has come down to us as the God-Man, i.e., God in human flesh, is the most meaningful that the ears of man have ever heard.

TRUTH AND WISDOM ARE IN THE INCARNATION

In the Incarnation, we have all truth and wisdom and knowledge in a warm, human form, pertinent, close, and comforting. "In whom [Jesus] are hid all the treasures of wisdom and knowledge," Paul wrote in Colossians 2:3.

What is God like? Look at Jesus. How shall we learn about the Lord? By sitting at the feet of the blessed Jesus. In Him the substance and revelation of God are revealed. Would a man know God? Let him know the Lord Jesus. Would a man follow God? Let him follow the Lord Jesus. Would a man worship God? Let him worship Jesus. Would a man love God? Let him love Jesus. Jesus is the revelation of all truth and righteouness and wisdom—the glory of God. For us He is precept, for He is the way. For us He is doctrine, for He is the truth. For us He is experience, for He is the life. If we would know God, we must look at Jesus.

No longer must we take down from the library shelf a dusty, dry, heavy tome and pour over its pages, reading those cabalistic, mysterious, double-meaning sentences to find the truth of the Almighty. We can just look to Jesus and there find revealed the fullness of the glory and meaning of God. We may be puzzled at the innumerable theories of the Atonement, but if we would know the forgiveness of sin, we have but to look to Jesus.

In my doctoral work one of my minors was the study of the Atonement. For two years, unceasingly, I studied the Atonement. I passed the examination on it in a room filled with learned professors. And when at the end of the two years I was given the doctor's degree, I knew no more how to explain the Atonement than when I began.

If you are puzzled by God's sacrifice for sin, just look to Jesus, trust in Jesus. You may stagger before those divine mysteries that concern theology and that overpower the minds of the greatest thinkers of the two thousand years of Christendom, but you can look to Jesus and trust in Him.

The Christian faith is above all other things an objective religion, an objective faith. It is out of ourselves and away from ourselves and looking at Jesus.

The Holy Spirit is our mentor and our instructor and His lesson is the Lord Jesus. He will not speak of Himself, but He reveals to us the glory of God in Christ Jesus (John 16:13).

Out of the years of experience of my own pastoral work, I have a word to say to every psychotic, neurotic, paranoid, and schizophrenic. Just forget about yourself. Quit thinking about yourself and look to Jesus. There is healing and salvation and life in the crucified One.

If you seek knowledge and wisdom, if you seek salvation and light, you can find it looking at Jesus.

> Turn your eyes upon Jesus,
> Look full in His wonderful face,
> And the things of earth
> Will grow strangely dim
> In the light of His glory and grace.

A New Dimension of God Is Seen in the Incarnation

In God's revelation of Himself in human form we see a new dimension of God. In Christ, He is revealed as our wonderful Savior, our tender and loving shepherd. That is especially cognitively emphatic against the background of the conception of God in most of the histories of the families of the earth. Elsewhere, and for the most part, God appears to be fierce.

In Calcutta, I remember standing in a temple before a man-made deity in the midst of a large group of worshipers. As I stood in their midst and looked at the god before whom they were bowing, I noted that the face of the god was terrible, his visage was horrible, his hands like claws, and his teeth bared in a terrible posture. I said to one of the Hindu worshipers there, "God is so fierce." He replied to me: "Indeed, and that is why I worship him. I am afraid of him."

Some of you have been in Bangkok and have observed all of the temples of those pagan gods. They are guarded by images that are extremely fierce. In the heart of central Africa, I went to see the king. Before his spacious compound, in which he lived with about thirty or forty of his wives and their children, there was a devil house where he worshiped the devil. I asked him why he had a house for worshiping the devil. He said to me: "I am afraid of him. He could do me harm."

Even in the revelation of God in the Old Testament, the number one attribute of Jehovah is holiness, perfection, and unapproachable righteousness. That separates us from God. In the beginning, because of sin, God drove Adam and Eve from His presence and out of the Garden of Eden. The God that was revealed as the administrator of the covenant of the law appeared to Moses in lightning and in thunder and in earthquakes—so much so that even if one chanced to touch the mountain, he died instantly.

In the later revelation of the worship of God in the temple, there was an outer wall to keep the people out. On the inside there was another wall to keep them out, and on the inside of that another wall to keep others out, and finally a door of the sanctuary to keep all of them out. On the inside of the sanctuary there was a veil behind which no one but the high priest could enter the innermost sanctuary of God and that only once a year with blood for atonement. The separation of the God of holiness from His people was ever apparent.

But in Christ Jesus we have a new dimension of the revelation of our Father in heaven. Consider Bethlehem where He became human flesh. Anyone would feel welcome and perfectly at home in the presence of a baby in a manger. Jesus was born in a cattle stall and surrounded by the flocks and herds of goats and cattle. Even the simple, humble shepherds glorified God in the presence of this gift from heaven.

In His ministry He took little children in His arms and blessed them. He preached the gospel of hope to the poor. He healed those who were sick. The common people heard Him gladly. The humanity of God in Christ Jesus is the greatest comfort we could ever know in our lives. Open your Bible to the Book of Hebrews and note these three passages that speak especially of the meaning of the humanity of God for us. He revealed Himself as our friend and our shepherd in Christ Jesus.

> For we have not a high priest which cannot be touched with the feeling of our infirmities; but was in all points tempted like as we are, yet without sin.
> Let us therefore come boldly unto the throne of grace, that we may obtain mercy, and find grace to help in time of need (Heb. 4:15–16).
>
> Wherefore in all things it behooved him to be made like unto his brethren, that he might be a merciful and faithful high priest in

110

things pertaining to God, to make reconciliation for the sins of the people.

For in that he himself hath suffered being tempted, he is able to succor them that are tempted (Heb. 2:17–18).

Our Lord chose to live a life like ours, knowing and experiencing it all, understanding every trial that we endure.

For ye are not come unto the mount that might be touched, and that burned with fire, nor unto blackness, and darkness, and tempest.

And the sound of a trumpet, and the voice of words; which voice they that heard entreated that the word should not be spoken to them any more:

(For they could not endure that which was commanded, And if so much as a beast touch the mountain, it shall be stoned, or thrust through with a dart:

And so terrible was the sight, that Moses said, I exceedingly fear and quake:)

But ye are come unto mount Zion, and unto the city of the living God, the heavenly Jerusalem, and to an innumerable company of angels,

To the general assembly and church of the first-born, which are written in heaven, and to God the Judge of all, and to the spirits of just men made perfect,

And to Jesus the mediator of the new covenant, and to the blood of sprinkling, that speaketh better things than of Abel (Heb. 12:18–24).

What the author of the Book of Hebrews is saying is that Christ sympathizes and understands every human experience that we have. Many a sufferer in a long night has found comfort in the presence of the Lord Jesus.

At the funeral service of my father I so well remember the pastor's words: "I went to see Mr. Criswell in the hospital where he died. I said to him, 'Mr. Criswell, how are you getting along?' And he replied, 'Pastor, the nights are long and lonely, but Jesus is with me.' "

How many an agonizing soul has been comforted with the remembrance of our Lord's intercession in Gethsemane. How many a martyr has clapped his hands with joy and sung praises of exaltation in remembering the crucifixion of our Lord. That is the meaning of the God-man for us—to sympathize, to understand, to help, to comfort, to be a fellow pilgrim with us in our journey from this world to the world that is to come.

ONLY GOD (REVEALED IN JESUS) CAN FORGIVE SIN

Jesus as God paid the sacrifice and atoning offering in order that we might be forgiven our sins. What or who can wash away sins? Who can wash the stain out of our souls so that we can appear spotless and without blemish in the presence of a holy and righteous God? Who can deliver us from the penalty, judgment, and death of sin? All the blood of bulls and goats that was ever poured out on all the sacrificial altars of the world could not wash away our sins. Shall I even offer my son or my daughter as a sacrifice for my sins? Do you remember the heart cry of Micah the prophet?

> Wherewith shall I come before the LORD, and bow myself before the high God? shall I come before him with burnt offerings, with calves of a year old?
> Will the LORD be pleased with thousands of rams, or with ten thousands of rivers of oil? shall I give my first-born for my transgression, the fruit of my body for the sin of my soul? (Micah 6:6–7).

Who can forgive sin and wash the stain of transgression out of our souls? Who? Can the greatest saints and leaders of the world, can those who in mighty power pass through the pages of the Bible and through human history, can they forgive our sins? Could Moses have died for me? Could David or Daniel or Samuel have died for me? Could the great saints of the New Covenant—Peter, James, John, Paul—could any one of them have died for me? Are there those in the heavenly angelic order who could make atonement for my sin? Could the archangels Michael or Gabriel have died for me? Who can make the atoning sacrifice for my sin?

It is because of who He is, it is the preeminence of His person that gives efficacy and power to the sacrifice of the Son of God. It is because He is God that He is able to atone for our sins. No one else could achieve the heavenly result. In our behalf, as the Scriptures say, our Lord tasted death for everyone. He died and paid the penalty for our sins.

No one can enter into the depths of the grief of Jesus as He suffered for us. No, not one. When Satan afflicted righteous Job, God allowed Satan to take away everything that Job had but refused to let the evil one lay his hand upon Job himself. But there was no interdiction and no reserve when Satan afflicted Jesus. They spit upon Him; they beat Him; they mocked and jeered Him; they crucified Him. Isaiah 52:14 says, "His visage was so marred more than any man." Isaiah 53:11 says, "[God] shall see of the travail of his soul." The holy, pure, and righteous Jesus suffered in His soul. I do not know how to comprehend it. God was making atonement for our sins that we might be delivered from the judgment of death and of hell, that we might be saved, that we might see God's face some day and live.

GOD LOST NOTHING OF HIS GLORY IN THE INCARNATION

The incarnation of God in Christ took away nothing of His glory. Rather His humanity, His condescension, His humiliation, His suffering have ministered to His greater glory. In John 17 we read that Christ had glory before the world was (v. 5). But this is an added glory. The glory that Jesus had in His preincarnate state was the incommunicable glory of deity—the unshared glory of God. But this glory is the glory of His humanity, a shared glory with the redeemed family of heaven for whom He paid His life, whom He bought with His own blood, and whom He counts as brothers and sisters in the household of faith.

That is why we praise Him and sing songs about Him and seek to serve Him all the days of our lives. Oh, what He has done for us—He adopted us as sinners into the holy, heavenly family of God. My brother, if the whole world were an alabaster box that includes heaven itself, He would be worthy to have it broken and its oil of perfume poured out upon Him alone!

Thus it is that people are blessed and life and light and salvation and elevation come to the soul who listens to the message of the preacher who preaches Christ. Not extraneous drivel, not the grinding out a tune of a pet economic or political persuasion, but preaching the lifting up of the Lord—that is the preacher's task!

Have you ever heard a Christian go out of a worship service saying: "The pastor preached too much about Jesus today. He exalted Christ too highly today. The pastor preached Jesus too joyfully, too zealously, too triumphantly, and too hopefully today"? Did you ever hear that? Did you ever stand at the door and see a Christian walk out of the congregation with a long, sad face and say: "You know, the pastor today exaggerated Jesus too much. He exalted the Lord too highly"? Did you ever hear of anyone who was sick and listening on the radio or watching on television who said: "You know today the pastor preached too much about Jesus. He had too many words of loving adoration about the Lord"? Did you ever know anyone who was bowed down with indescribable sorrow and grief who said: "I am bitter because the pastor came and brought me a loving promise from Him who said, 'I will never leave thee nor forsake thee' "?

Somehow preaching Christ is life and salvation and hope and heaven. "And I, if I be lifted up from the earth, will draw all men unto me" (John 12:32).

> If Jesus Christ is a man,
>   And only a man, I say,
> That of all mankind I will follow Him,
>   And him will I follow alway.
>
> But if Jesus Christ is a God,
>   And the only God, I swear,
> I will follow Him through heaven and hell,
>   The earth, the sea, and the air!

This is the meaning for us of the God-man, Christ Jesus. He is our Savior and our Lord forever.

12

Our Lord's Entrance Into Human Flesh

The avowal that begins the Gospel of John reads like this: "In the beginning was the *Logos*," translated "the Word." That is a philosophical term referring to the active reason of God, the God who moves, who acts, who creates, who comes to visit men.

> In the beginning was the Word, and the Word was with God, and the Word was God.
> And the Word [*Logos*], was made flesh [entered human life], and dwelt among us, (and we beheld his glory, the glory as of the only begotten of the Father,) full of grace and truth.
> For the law was given by Moses, but grace and truth came by Jesus Christ (John 1:1, 14, 17).

From the beginning the heraldic announcement (*kerugma*) of the gospel was that God was made manifest in human flesh. God was incarnate in Jesus Christ. He came into the world in a body in order to make atoning sacrifice for the sins of mankind. He was in Christ reconciling the world unto Himself, not imputing unto us our own sins. He was made sin for us, Him who knew no sin, that we might be made the righteousness of God in Him. This was the heart and the soul of the simple gospel preached by the apostles.

THE GOSPEL WAS DENIED AND PERVERTED

From the beginning, even in the days of the apostles, the gospel was denied and diluted. Heretical sophistry entered into the preaching of the gospel. These so-called intellectuals—

gnostics and sophists—denied the Incarnation, the Virgin Birth, and the Resurrection.

The background of that gnostic heresy is seen again and again in the New Testament. It was pervasive; it was everywhere. Gnosticism assumed in most of its development a docetic form or a Cerinthian form. Let us first look at Docetic Gnosticism. The Greek word for "know" is *gnōsis,* and thus we get the term "gnostic." *Dokeō,* meaning "to seem," gives us the term "docetic." Docetic Gnosticism proclaimed that Christ never had an actual body; rather He had only an apparent body. They said that it was impossible for God to become human flesh. The Docetic Gnostics maintained that Jesus just appeared to have flesh and bones.

The Cerinthian Gnostics were named after Cerinthus, who was John the apostle's bitter enemy in Ephesus. Cerinthus said that the power of God came upon Jesus at His baptism and then left Him at the cross. Cerinthus denied that Jesus was incarnate God. He denied the Virgin Birth. He denied the bodily resurrection. This is the heretical background against which the gospel was preached throughout the Graeco-Roman world. The apostles in their defense of the faith never swerved from that gospel of the duality of the person of Christ. God of very God and man of very man—the God-man, Christ Jesus.

Paul writes to Timothy, his son in the ministry.

> O Timothy, keep that which is committed to thy trust, avoiding profane and vain babblings, and oppositions of science [gnoticism] falsely so called (1 Tim. 6:20).

The sainted apostle John wrote this warning:

> For many deceivers are entered into the world, who confess not that Jesus Christ is come in the flesh [that He has body and bones]. This is a deceiver and an antichrist (2 John 7).

That Greek participle *erchomai,* translated "come," can refer either to His first coming (the Gnostics denied that God was incarnate and that He was born of a virgin), or it can refer to His second coming (the Gnostics also denied that Jesus Christ is coming visibly in the flesh with a body). Whether His first coming or His second coming, the Gnostics denied the physical manifestation of God in human flesh.

MODERN GNOSTICISM

The modern Gnostics are no different. The heresy that confronted the apostles in their day is the same heresy that sweeps the entire world of Christendom today. It is in the pulpit everywhere. It is in the theological chairs throughout the academic world. It apparently is the acceptable philosophical explanation of the Christian faith today. Gnosticism—a superior, intellectual approach to the gospel of Christ—denies the Virgin Birth, the bodily Resurrection, and the visible, personal, physical return of our Lord to the earth. The Gnostics refuse to accept the humanity of Jesus. They will not acknowledge Him as the God-man.

When I was preaching through the Bible, I remember well coming to Luke 24. I was in the center of that chapter, which unfolds the story of the appearance of the risen, resurrected, glorified Lord to His apostles.

> And as they thus spake, Jesus himself stood in the midst of them, and saith unto them, Peace be unto you.
> But they were terrified and affrighted, and supposed that they had seen a spirit.
> And he said unto them, Why are ye troubled? and why do thoughts arise in your hearts?
> Behold my hands and my feet, that it is I myself: handle me, and see; for a spirit hath not flesh and bones, as ye see me have.
> And when he had thus spoken, he showed them his hands and his feet.
> And while they yet believed not for joy, and wondered, he said unto them, Have ye here any meat?
> And they gave him a piece of a broiled fish, and of a honeycomb.
> And he took it, and did eat before them (Luke 24:36–43).

As I expounded that passage concerning the actual physical bodily resurrection of Jesus our Lord that Sunday, a modern Gnostic, i.e., an intellectual who denied the Virgin Birth, the Incarnation, and the bodily Resurrection of our Lord, was in the congregation. As he went out of the church service, he said to a friend: "Such a sermon! How grossly material and how unbelievably and crudely physical!" You see, the Christ that our modern Gnostics preach was never incarnate God. The Christ they preach was not born of a virgin. The Christ they preach never rose bodily from the dead. The Christ they preach never ascended bodily into heaven. And certainly the Christ that they preach will never come again visibly and personally. The Christ that they preach is a metaphysical speculation; He is an immaterial ghost; He is a philosophical opinion. He is merely an idea, a thought, an intellectual presupposition.

Imagine a man saying,

> I believe in the spiritual, intellectual idea of George Washington, but I do not believe in the physical existence of the man himself. I do not believe in a George Washington who was born in Westmoreland County, Virginia, in 1732. I do not believe in a George Washington who married Martha Custis, who lived at Mount Vernon, who led the Revolutionary War, whose ideas framed the Constitution of the United States, and who was elected the first president of the Republic. I do not believe in a physical George Washington, but I believe in a spiritual George Washington whose ideas pervaded the colonies in their Puritan days and whose ideas are among us now.

They are rationalists without reason; they are thinkers without thought; they are logicians without logic.

THE SCRIPTURES BEAR WITNESS TO HIS DUALITY

With unswerving unanimity the Scriptures bear witness to the duality of the person of Christ. He was God of very God, God incarnate, and He was man of very man, a human being like us. The scriptural presentation of the duality of Christ is a marvelous thing to behold in the revelation of the goodness of God.

In the Old Testament, there is a wonderful and beautiful figure who appears again and again in bodily form. He is a theophonic angel. He is the angel of Jehovah. He is the angel of the presence of the face of God. He appears in the Old Covenant bodily to Jacob at Peniel and to Joshua before Jericho, introducing Himself as the Captain of the hosts of the armies of God. He introduces Himself as the Lord Jehovah to Isaiah who saw Him high and lifted up. He introduces Himself as the Ancient of Days to Daniel. In the Old Covenant there is this marvelous and glorious figure who appears again and again.

At the consummation of the age, that same glorious figure appears. In the first chapter of the Apocalypse, the sainted John describes Him as he looked upon Him walking in the midst of the seven golden lampstands in the midst of His churches.

> And in the midst of the seven candlesticks one like unto the Son of man, clothed with a garment down to the foot, and girt about the paps with a golden girdle.
>
> His head and his hairs were white like wool, as white as snow; and his eyes were as a flame of fire;
>
> And his feet like unto fine brass, as if they burned in a furnace; and his voice as the sound of many waters.
>
> And he had in his right hand seven stars: and out of his mouth went a sharp two-edged sword: and his countenance was as the sun shineth in his strength.
>
> And when I saw him, I fell at his feet as dead (Rev. 1:13–18a).

In the ages before, preexistent and eternal, and in the ages to come we see the same marvelous, glorified Christ Jesus. The brief valley in between holds the days of His flesh, His humiliation and suffering, when He was presented to us as the lowly and precious Lord Jesus. That is the Bible, the revelation of God, the gospel the apostles preached. With great unanimity the Scriptures witnessed to that duality in Christ. He is God of very God and man of very man—the God-man, God incarnate.

In Isaiah 9, we read this beautiful, incomparable prophecy:

> For unto us a child is born, unto us a son is given: and the government shall be upon his shoulder: and his name shall be called Wonderful, Counselor, The mighty God, The everlasting Father, The Prince of Peace (v. 6).

Look at the duality in that marvelous prophecy. "For unto us a child is born." The prophet directs us to His humanity. He introduces us to the wonderful child, and he takes us to Bethlehem and the stable and the manger. Then he takes us to the desert with its hunger. He takes us to the well of water with its thirst. He takes us to the sea with its midnight storm. He takes us to the carpenter's shop with its daily toil. He takes us to Gethsemane where He agonized in soul. He takes us to Golgotha where He died a malefactor's death in His humanity. He takes us to the grave where He was buried. "Unto us a child is born"—this is His humanity.

But there is more—"Unto us a son is given." He was a Son before He was born. The prophet conducts us now to heaven, to the preexistent, coeternal Christ, whose name He says is Wonderful, Counselor, The mighty God, The everlasting Father, The Prince of Peace. The duality is clearly seen in the Scriptures.

Paul quotes a hymn out of the church and writes,

> And without controversy great is the mystery of godliness: God
> was manifest in the flesh, justified in the Spirit, seen of angels,
> preached unto the Gentiles, believed on in the world, received up
> into glory (1 Tim. 3:16a).

Paul loves that word "manifest" (*phaneroō*), a reference to a
preexistent person who is presented to us and manifested to us
now. It is a mystery that overwhelms us—that God should be
man and dwell among us.

The Book of Hebrews speaks of God who is the express
image of the Father, who is the brightness of His glory (Heb.
1:1–3). That same glorious God is given a body that He might
make sacrifice, pouring out His life and blood for our sins (Heb.
10:5). He is described as a faithful High Priest, sympathetic with
us, tried in all points like as we are, though without sin (Heb.
2:17–18). We are told to come boldly to His throne that we
might find grace to help in time of need (Heb. 4:15–16). Always
there is that duality, the glorious God in human life.

Thus it was that the apostle Peter wrote in the same vein:

> Who verily was foreordained before the foundation of the
> world, but was manifest [*phaneroō*] in these last times for you
> (1 Pet. 1:20).

The great eternal, preexistent God is manifest to us now in order
that we might be saved.

That same glorious message is repeated again by the apostle
John.

> For this purpose the Son of God was manifested [there is that
> word again, *phaneroō*, the eternal *Logos* was made flesh and we
> looked upon him], that he might destroy [*luō*, meaning "to break
> up"] the works of the devil (1 John 3:8b).

God came into the world and was made manifest that He might
break up the house of Satan and the works of the devil.

The apostle John writes in this same vein as he introduces
his first epistle:

> That which was from the beginning, which we have heard,
> which we have seen with our eyes, which we have looked upon,
> and our hands have handled, of the Word [*Logos*] of life;
> (For the life was manifested [it assumed flesh], and we have
> seen it, and bear witness, and show unto you that eternal life, which
> was with the Father, and was manifested [*phaneroō*] unto us;)
> That which we have seen and heard declare we unto you, that

ye also may have fellowship with us: and truly our fellowship is with
the Father, and with his Son Jesus Christ (1 John 1:1–4).

The apostles knew Christ in the same way that a chemist
knows salt or a geologist knows rocks or an astronomer knows
stars. They knew Christ, they heard Him, they listened to Him,
they saw Him, they touched Him, they lived with Him. They bore
witness to this living Lord in His birth of a virgin, in His life as a
preacher of the good news of the gospel, in His death and burial,
in His glorious Resurrection, in His Ascension into Heaven, and
in His promise to come again. That is the gospel. That is the
witness of the Word. That is the manifest revelation of God.

In His birth, in His Incarnation, the Lord Christ was flesh and
bones. In His ministry, He was a man preaching the gospel, a
man with flesh and bones. In His death He was a man with flesh
and bones, crucified. In His burial He was a dead man of flesh
and bones. In His Resurrection He was the same man with flesh
and bones raised from the dead and glorified. In His ascension
into heaven, He was a man with flesh and bones, glorified and
resurrected. In His great mediatorial capacity as our High Priest,
the God of glory is a man with flesh and bones, God incarnate.
One of these glorious days it will be that same Lord Jesus, a man
with flesh and bones, whom we shall see visibly and personally
coming down in triumph and in glory in the *shekinah* cloud,
"and every eye shall see him"—the same Lord Jesus.

If we depart from the historical Christ, we depart from the
gospel itself and empty the Christian faith of its very definition.
Just as there is no Jesus who was not born of a Virgin Mary, just
as there is no Jesus who was not bodily raised from the dead, just
so there is no such thing as a Jesus who will not bodily, physi-
cally, and personally descend from the skies. The church is looking upward, not like a star gazer, not like one examining an al-
manac, but the church is looking up in great expectation. The
face of the church is heavenward and Christward, believing God
has prepared some better thing for us. We are looking for Jesus,
not for a ghost, not for an apparition, not for a philosophical idea,
not for some metaphysical hope or persuasion. We are looking
for Jesus, the God-man, our wonderful Savior, King of the earth,
Captain of the hosts of heaven, the atoning lover of our souls. He
writes our names in the Book of Life, He is our companion and
fellow pilgrim in the journey through this world; He is our great

friend in the hour of death, and He waits to receive us into heaven. That is Jesus, the God-man, Christ Jesus. That is the gospel of the Bible. It is the gospel of Peter and Paul and John. It is our gospel in which we have found hope and refuge today.

A beloved physician in our church sent me a little note and enclosed with it a poem that avows the truth that I have tried to expound on the duality of the person of Christ as God and man.

> Our blessed Lord combined in one, two natures, both complete;
> A perfect manhood all sublime, in Godhead all replete.
>
> As man He entered Cana's feast, a humble guest to dine;
> As God He moved the water there, and changed it into wine.
>
> As man He climbed the mountain's height, a suppliant to be;
> As God He left the place of prayer and walked upon the sea.
>
> As man He wept in heartfelt grief, beside a loved one's grave;
> As God He burst the bands of death, Almighty still to save.
>
> As man He lay within a boat o'erpowered by needful sleep;
> As God He rose, rebuked the wind and stilled the angry deep.
>
> Such was our Lord in life on earth, in dual nature one;
> The woman's seed in very truth and God's eternal Son.
>
> O Child, O Son, O Word made flesh, may Thy high praise increase:
> Called Wonderful, The Mighty God, Eternal Prince of Peace.

That is the gospel. This is the God who died for us, who saved us, who will raise us from the dead, who is coming for us, and who has prepared a place for us in heaven. His name is Jesus our Lord—God in the flesh. That is the most precious gospel that mind could imagine—that God is Christ, touchable to us, moved with the feeling of our infirmities, knowing all about us, still loving us and saving us, keeping us, bowing down His ear to listen and hearing us when we pray, living in our hearts, waiting for us in heaven! Oh, that we could sing about that marvelous gospel and praise this glorious Savior, our Lord Jesus, in a way worthy of His precious name!

13

Our Lord's Entrance Into Suffering

> But we see Jesus, who was made a little lower than the angels for the suffering of death, crowned with glory and honor; that he by the grace of God should taste death for every man.
>
> For it became him, for whom are all things, and by whom are all things, in bringing many sons unto glory, to make the captain of their salvation perfect through sufferings.
>
> Forasmuch then as the children are partakers of flesh and blood, he also himself likewise took part of the same; that through death he might destroy him that had the power of death, that is, the devil;
>
> And deliver them who through fear of death were all their lifetime subject to bondage (Heb. 2:9, 10, 14, 15).

The text here is so descriptive of our Lord. He was made a little lower than the angels, made a man, made like us that by the grace of God He should taste death for every man. In bringing many sons unto glory, the captain of our salvation was made perfect through suffering.

> Who in the days of his flesh, when he had offered up prayers and supplications with strong crying and tears unto him that was able to save him from death, and was heard in that he feared;
>
> Though he were a Son, yet learned he obedience by the things which he suffered;
>
> And being made perfect, he became the author of eternal salvation unto all them that obey him (Heb. 5:7-8).

By the grace of God the Captain of our salvation was made "perfect" through suffering. Though He was a son, yet He learned obedience by the things He suffered; and being made "perfect," He became the author of eternal salvation for all of us who will accept Him. To us the word "perfect" means sinless, moral perfection. But it has no connotation like that in the word translated "perfect" (*teleios*).

This word *teleios* refers to a purpose for which a thing was made as being fulfilled. For example, an oak tree is the *teleios* of an acorn. An acorn was made to grow into a tree. So the tree is the *teleios* of the acorn, having achieved the purpose for which the acorn was made. A man is the *teleios* of a boy. If the lad stayed a boy, it would be tragic. He would be stunted. He would not reach the goal for which God made him.

That word is applied to our Lord Christ: it pleased God to make the Captain of our salvation "perfect" through suffering. Though He were a son learning obedience by the things that He suffered, He was made *teleios,* having accomplished the purpose that God planned for Him. He came into the world to suffer and to die in order that having achieved the purpose or *teleios,* He would be the author of an eternal salvation for us who receive His loving grace and the pardon of our sins in Him.

Our Lord Arrives at the Day of His Suffering

In Hebrews 10, there is a magnificent discussion of the purpose (*teleios*) that our Lord achieved for us.

> For it is not possible that the blood of bulls and of goats should take away sins (Heb. 10:4).

Every time sacrifices are made, we are reminded of our sins, according to the author of Hebrews. The sacrifices had to be repeated again and again because they were not able to wash away sins. But our Lord was sacrificed once for all. There is power in the blood.

> Wherefore when he cometh into the world, he saith, Sacrifice and offering thou wouldest not, but a body hast thou prepared me:
>
> Then said I, Lo, I come (in the volume of the book it is written of me) to do thy will, O God (Heb. 10:5, 7).

He came into the world to fulfill the purpose of God for His life—to suffer, to die that we might be saved.

The gospel poignantly describes the agony of soul in which our Lord faced those days for which He came. As He stood at the threshold of the purpose (*teleios*) to be achieved, i.e., the assignment to suffer, He did it with distress and agony.

In the Gospel of Luke our Lord says,

> But I have a baptism to be baptized with; and how am I straitened [i.e., distressed, in agony] till it be accomplished (12:50).

When the Greeks came to see Him, as recorded in John, it brought to His mind the imminent offering of Himself in suffering for the sins of the whole world.

> Now is my soul troubled; and what shall I say? Father, save me from this hour: but for this cause came I unto this hour (John 12:27).

In Matthew 26, when the disciples sought to defend Him, He said to Simon Peter:

> Put up again thy sword into his place: for all they that take the sword shall perish with the sword.
> Thinkest thou that I cannot now pray to my Father, and he shall presently give me more than twelve legions of angels?
> But how then shall the scriptures be fulfilled, that thus it must be? (vv. 52–54).

He could have had 72,000 angels standing by His side, but then how would the purpose of God be realized and the scriptural announcement of His coming into the world to die for sins be fulfilled?

> Father, if thou be willing, remove this cup from me: nevertheless not my will, but thine, be done.
> And there appeared an angel unto him from heaven, strengthening him.
> And being in an agony he prayed more earnestly: and his sweat was as it were great drops of blood falling down to the ground (Luke 22:42–44).

As our Lord entered into His assignment to suffer for our sins, He did so in agony of soul.

In the remarkable prophecy of Isaiah 53, perhaps the greatest prophecy in the Old Testament, the prophet says:

> Yet it pleased the LORD to bruise him; he hath put him to grief: when thou shalt make his soul an offering for sin,
> He shall see of the travail of his soul, and shall be satisfied (vv. 10a, 11a).

God will receive His sacrifice as being sufficient to wash away all our sins.

The prophecy, "God shall see the travail of his soul and shall be satisfied," is beyond my understanding. The travail of the soul of Jesus—God shall make His soul an offering for sin—this is difficult to comprehend. I can understand the crucifixion by reading and by picture, but I do not know how to enter into the travail of soul. As the Lord faced His assignment in suffering, He did so in an agony of spirit that is beyond our comprehension or understanding.

He lived in heaven, where the brightness of holiness resides. But the earth is so filled with death, disease, despair, sorrow, and tears. It must have been a choice of tremendous agony to leave so beautiful a kingdom and to come down to so dark an earth. He did so because we are here, we who are in the agony of death, tears, and sorrow.

Look at Jesus as the Crown Prince of glory. Consider Him as the object of worship of all the angels of heaven.

> And again, when he bringeth in the first begotten into the world, he saith, and let all the angels of God worship him (Heb. 1:6).

So beautiful, resplendent, irridescent, and brilliant was the worship of Jesus in heaven that even Satan, the archangel with whom God entrusted the created world, envied Him. Seeing Jesus as the One before whom all heaven bowed, that sin of pride arose in his heart and led to the destruction of God's universe.

On the other hand, can we imagine the agony of His spirit when they bowed the knee before Him in mockery, saying, "Hail, King of the Jews"? Can we imagine the crown of thorns that was placed on His head or the scepter made from a cheap reed and placed in His hand or the castoff garment placed on His back as a robe? He who had been the object of the adoration of all the hosts of heaven was now mocked and abused! What agony of soul! I cannot enter into it.

The face of the Son of God is the light and the glory of heaven. They have no need for the sun or the moon, for the light of the Lamb is the brightness of heaven. His face shone as the sun in its splendor. Can you imagine the agony of soul when they covered His face with spittle or when they plucked out His beard or when they smote Him with their hands? The agony of soul of Him who set upon the throne of glory, the God who created the world and who is now nailed to a tree!

In ancient times they impaled their victims. That was their form of execution. In impaling, the victim died immediately. But on the cross, the victim remained for hours and even for days.

The Purpose and Achievement of His Suffering

The author of Hebrews gives three things concerning the suffering of Christ. First, He suffered in order that He might be identified with us and be made one with us.

> For both he that sancifieth [makes us holy] and they who are sanctified are all of one: for which cause he is not ashamed to call them brethren,
> Forasmuch then as the children are partakers of flesh and blood, he also himself likewise took part of the same; that through death he might destroy him that had the power of death, that is, the devil;
> For verily he took not on him the nature of angels; but he took on him the seed of Abraham [the likeness of a man].
> Wherefore in all things it behooved him to be made like unto his brethren, that he might be a merciful and faithful high priest in things pertaining to God, to make reconciliation for the sins of the people.
> For in that he himself hath suffered being tempted, he is able to succor them that are tempted (Heb. 2:11, 14, 16–18).

The first purpose then for the coming of our Lord into the world to suffer was to identify Himself with us. As I think of that, over the long years of my pastoral experience, I do not know of a more common denominator of human life than tears and sorrows and suffering. The common denominator of life is not richness because so many of us are poor. It is not strength and health because so many of us are sick. There is not anything that I know of like the common denominator of suffering, sorrow, and tears. For example, consider the matter of tears as they might affect us in a variety of ways. When the child cries, we say those are childish tears. However, to the child, they are as real as the tears of adults. The broken-heartedness, the disappointment, the hurt, and the sorrow of a child are very real. Consider the tears of teenagers, which express the poignancy of some of the hurt that they go through. Their tears are real. Different still are the tears of manhood and womanhood; the disappointments, the frustrations, the broken dreams that we know in life sometimes crush our souls. The tears of separation, loneliness, old age, and death sometimes bring us to despair.

Jesus came to be made like one of us that we might be one with Him. Had He come into this world as a kingly prince living in a palace with a golden crown and a diamond scepter, how many of us would have felt comfortable in His presence? Had He come into this world as the head of the hosts of brilliant angels, how many of us would have felt that He understands us? But having come into the world poor, the friend of sinners, the meek, the lonely, the hungry, the thirsty, we somehow find Him as our brother. He came to identify Himself with us.

In His obedience, the Scriptures say, though He were a son, He learned submissiveness, carrying out the will of God (Heb. 5:8–9). In so many ways do we need to be taught to be submissive in the harsh providences of life. In submission, Job said:

> Naked came I out of my mother's womb, and naked shall I return thither: the LORD gave, and the LORD hath taken away; blessed be the name of the LORD (Job 1:21).

> Shall we receive good at the hand of God, and shall we not receive evil? In all this did not Job sin with his lips (Job 2:10b).

We see the submissive spirit of our Savior in His words,

> The cup which my Father hath given me, shall I not drink it? (John 18:11b).

In His suffering, the Lord is our great sympathizing High Priest. The author of Hebrews says it so beautifully,

> For we have not an high priest which cannot be touched with the feeling of our infirmities; but was in all points tempted like as we are, yet without sin.
> Let us therefore come boldly unto the throne of grace, that we may obtain mercy, and find grace to help in time of need (4:15–16).

He knows all about the sorrow, the frustration, the disappointments, and the tears of our lives. Though He is God, He is our brother. That was the first purpose, the author states, of His coming into the world: that He might identify Himself with us, to be one of us.

The second reason, the author says, for His coming into the world and the purpose (*teleios*) or the achievement of His life was to deliver us from the bondage of death.

> But we see Jesus, who was made a little lower than the angels for the suffering of death, crowned with glory and honor; that he by the grace of God should taste death for every man.
> And deliver them who through fear of death were all their lifetime subject to bondage (Heb. 2:9, 15).

All of us have a twofold dread of death. We fear death instinctively. That fear we have in common with all of the animal kingdom. There is no creature that does not seek to escape death by running or fighting. Instinctively we dread the awesome approach of death.

We have another fear of death and that is the uncertainty of what lies beyond death. If one will think of it, it is frightening. What lies in that dark corridor beyond the River Styx, as the Greeks would philosophize about it, beyond *sheol* and its shades, as the Hebrews would say it? What is ahead? What lies beyond the gates of death? Our Savior came to deliver us from that bondage and fear. Because of His victory over death and the grave, we now do not experience death. We are just translated through the open door into heaven. It is God's way of receiving us into paradise. Flesh and blood cannot inherit the kingdom of heaven. As long as I am in this house of clay, I cannot even see God's face and live. Because of Jesus' atoning sacrifice, the victory of Christ means death is but the gate into heaven.

How are those gates wrought and of what are they made? They are gates of pearl, and a pearl is the only gem made out of the hurt and the wound of a little animal. Death is the gate into paradise, into heaven, and it is made out of pearl. Through suffering we enter into the kingdom of God.

During a crusade in Odessa, Texas, a pastor took me to a little coffee shop. While he and I were visiting together, a blind man entered the coffee shop. He came over and sat down close to us, and the pastor said to me, "I want you to listen to that blind man as he prays." Before the man ate, he said the blessing aloud. The pastor said to me, "Every time that blind man prays, he thanks God for his blindness." He went on to explain that before the man was blinded, he had been a very wicked man, but in his blindness he was led to the Lord.

My brothers and sisters, God has some holy purpose for every sorrow that we experience in life. God purposes some beautiful thing for us in it. Instead of rebelling and becoming bitter, let us accept whatever God sends in His providence, and be humbled by it and learn to lean upon the kind arm of God for strength. What is heaven like? It is described as being a place where there is no more death or sorrow or crying. Neither will there be any more pain or tears, for these things have all passed away. What would that mean to someone who had never cried? What would that mean to someone who had never suffered? What would that mean to someone whose heart had never been broken? What would that mean to someone who had never faced death? It is in these providences of God in which our Savior is a brother that we come to know the riches of the depth and the height and the breadth of the love of God in Christ Jesus. That is why He came to suffer.

There is a third reason for His suffering:

> But we see Jesus, who was made a little lower than the angels for the suffering of death, crowned with glory and honor; that he by the grace of God should taste death for every man.
>
> For it became him, for whom are all things, and by whom are all things, in bringing many sons unto glory, to make the captain of their salvation perfect through sufferings (Heb. 2:9–10).

Do you see the imagery of that? The great throng that our Lord is leading into heaven is a throng that He has saved by virtue of His tears, suffering, and death. It is a sainted throng that He is leading into glory. Every pilgrim company must have a "Great Heart." Every army must have a general or a captain. Every exodus must have a Moses. Leading the saints of God into heaven, we have the great Savior and Captain of our salvation.

In Ephesians we read about a magnificent imagery comparing the entrance of our Lord with His people into heaven to a Roman triumph.

> When he ascended up on high, he led captivity captive, and gave gifts unto men (4:8).

Satan is chained to his chariot wheels, and accompanying the Lord into glory are the saints He has won, the people for whom He has died, the souls whom He has saved. In that great throng going into heaven there are the sinners, the blind, the crippled,

130

the hurt, the sorrowing, the weeping, the repentant. These are the saints whom the Lord is taking with Him into glory.

In my reading, I came across something that blessed my heart. It is about an American doctor. Though his name is not given in the book, his funeral is described. The article said that when he was buried, the funeral carriage that carried him was attended by sixty pallbearers, each one of whom owed his life to that beloved physician. Behind the pallbearer's carriages walked eight hundred men, all of whom owed their ability to walk to the ministries of that beloved doctor. An additional 293 carriages followed. This was not the funeral of a great military hero or a political genius, but it was the memorial service of a man of God who had poured his life into the healing of the people. That is going to be the way it is when God leads His saints marching into heaven. These are they whom He has lifted out of the gutter. These are they whom He has pardoned from their sins. These are they to whom He has given strength, health, hope, life, and salvation. They are going to follow our Lord into heaven. The author here speaks of it as "leading many sons into glory."

O Lord, what a wonderful, incomparably precious thing God has done in sending us His beloved and only Son! Identified with us, sympathizing with us, taking away from us the fear of the agony of death, and opening for us the gates of glory through which one day we shall follow Him, marching into heaven!

14

The Awesome Mystery
of the Atonement

> For when we were yet without strength, in due time Christ died for the ungodly.
>
> For scarcely for a righteous man will one die: yet peradventure for a good man some would even dare to die.
>
> But God commendeth his love toward us, in that, while we were yet sinners, Christ died for us.
>
> Much more then, being now justified by his blood, we shall be saved from wrath through him.
>
> For if, when we were enemies, we were reconciled to God by the death of his Son, much more, being reconciled, we shall be saved by his life.
>
> And not only so, but we also joy in God through our Lord Jesus Christ, by whom we have now received the atonement (Rom. 5:6–11).

There have been literally libraries of books written concerning the atonement of Christ and how the death of Christ saves us from our sins. They are filled with theological language and philosophical discussions. We can read these many human speculations and attempts to explain the deep, unfathomable mysteries of God. But it does not help us if I stand here and try to repeat the theological, philosophical, theoretical, hypothetical reasons why Christ died. What we need is something that we can see and experience. How does the atonement of Christ affect me? What is God doing that I can understand, feel, and experience and to which I can respond in my heart?

The Awesome Mystery of the Atonement

There is a universal law in which all of us share. It is everywhere. There is no family, tribe, or people so degraded or so low that they are not morally sensitive. That is how God created us, and we are created in His image. This does not refer to our intellectual capacities. There are many animals that are shrewd and intelligent. The image of God in us refers to our moral sensitivity. In the vast panorama of creation, we are the only ones who possess that image and moral sensitivity. The entire human race of all generations has felt that moral lack, the condemnation of sin and transgression, the burden of guilt. How do we get rid of it? How do we face it? What do we do with it?

Look at this dramatic and poignant presentation in the Revelation.

> And the heaven departed as a scroll when it is rolled together; and every mountain and island were moved out of their places.
> And the kings of the earth, and the great men, and the rich men, and the chief captains, and the mighty men, and every bondman, and every free man, hid themselves in the dens and in the rocks of the mountains;
> And said to the mountains and rocks, Fall on us, and hide us from the face of him that sitteth on the throne, and from the wrath of the Lamb:
> For the great day of his wrath is come; and who shall be able to stand? (6:14–17).

Can rocks and mountains hide us from the judgment day of almighty God? Do rocks and mountains cover our transgressions? All generations have felt in their souls that sense of guilt and condemnation because of their sins. That is our moral sensitivity.

Adam and Eve, in their transgression, sewed fig leaves together and made aprons to cover their nakedness. Why was that insufficient? Why were the fig leaves unable to cover them? When they heard the voice of the Lord God as He came to visit, Adam and Eve hid themselves and were afraid. They were ashamed because they were naked. Having done all they knew to do to hide their sin, nakedness, and shame, they were still vulnerable and afraid.

We are told that when Ahab went out to battle, he made himself armor and covered his entire body to protect himself in the hour of battle. However, an enemy soldier drew his bow and let fly the arrow at a venture (i.e., he did not aim it, but just let the arrow fly). The arrow found a crevice in the king's armor and pierced his heart. The crimson of his life flowed out in the chariot, and he died according to the saying of the man of God. Can we build armor to preserve ourselves from the darts of our moral condemnation?

Perhaps the most dramatic of all of the dramas ever written is that of Macbeth. Encouraged by Lady Macbeth, the thane took a dagger and plunged it into the heart of the guest in his own castle. He murdered Duncan, king of Scotland. When he came back to Lady Macbeth, his hand was bathed in the blood from the dagger. Lady Macbeth said to her husband: "Go wash your hands. A little clean water will clear us of this deed." As Macbeth made his way to the fountain in the palace to wash his hands, he said:

> Will all great Neptune's ocean
> Wash this blood clean from my hand?
> No: this my hand will the multitudinous seas incarnadine,
> Making the green one, red.

How do you wash the blood of guilt from your hands?

A judge is seated on the bench, and before him is his own teenage son. Surely being the son of the judge will clear the boy of the wrong that he has done. But the judge, looking at the boy who stands in front of him, opens the statutes of the law, and he has no other choice but to read the condemnation.

The sense of moral lack and depravity is universal. We are a fallen and dying humanity—fallen in mind, heart, will, and life.

GOD'S PROVISION FOR REDEMPTION

There is also another universal law. It is the law of redemption, repurchase, and ransom. We read in Leviticus 25 that if the possessions of a poor man were taken away from him, the law of redemption or ransom said that a kinsman could buy back his poor brother's loss.

In that same chapter, if the poor man had sold himself into slavery, a kinsman could buy him back and redeem him. Any slave could be bought back, redeemed, and freed in an exchange of money. The law of redemption or ransom is universal.

An amazing discovery I have made in my study is related to the word translated "atonement" or "reconciliation."

> For if, when we were enemies, we were reconciled to God by the death of his Son, much more, being reconciled, we shall be saved by his life.
>
> And not only so, but we also joy in God through our Lord Jesus Christ, by whom we have now received the atonement [This is the only place in the New Testament where the word "reconciliation" is translated "atonement"] (Rom. 5:10–11).

Look at it again as Paul writes:

> And all things are of God, who hath reconciled us to himself by Jesus Christ, and hath given to us the ministry of reconciliation;
>
> To wit [namely], that God was in Christ, reconciling the world unto himself, not imputing their trespasses unto them; and hath committed unto us the word of reconciliation.
>
> Now then we are ambassadors for Christ, as though God did beseech you by us: we pray you in Christ's stead, be ye reconciled to God (2 Cor. 5:18–20).

The word translated "be ye reconciled" (*katallagēte*) and the word "reconciliation" (*katallagēs*), translated in one place "atonement," originally meant an exchange, as an exchange of money. It came to be reconciliation because it described the exchange of enmity for friendship or of hatred for love. It is used here to describe what Christ has done for us. He bought us. He redeemed us. He paid the ransom for us.

Look at that universally. Two armies are battling each other. One side has captured a general from the other side, and that side says, "We will exchange this general for give hundred private soldiers." Or, "We have captured a captain, and we will exchange (*katallassō*) this captain for ten private soldiers."

Someone has a big, beautiful diamond. "I will exchange this diamond for thousands of dollars that I owe you in debt." He wishes to exchange one for thousands.

A rich man is able to pay the debt of thousands of poor people who are facing the confiscation of their homes or farms. He is able to pay the debt because he is rich.

So Christ is thus described in His deity. In His incomparable, indescribable, immeasurable, unfathomable, life, soul, being, love, grace, goodness, loving-kindness, and friendship, Christ exchanges His self and His love in sacrifice. He vicariously gives of Himself. He does that to purchase for Himself all of us who are poor, undone sinners facing slavery and condemnation and judgment. That is why Paul says,

> . . . .Ye are not your own.
> For ye are bought with a price: therefore glorify God in your
> body, and in your spirit, which are God's (1 Cor. 6:19b–20).

That is why Simon Peter writes in the first chapter of his first
letter,

> Forasmuch as ye know that ye were not redeemed with cor-
> ruptible things, as silver and gold, from your vain conversation re-
> ceived by tradition from your father;
> But with the precious blood of Christ, as of a lamb without
> blemish and without spot (vv. 18–19).

That is why the Lord said,

> Even as the Son of man came not to be ministered unto, but to
> minister, and to give his life a ransom for many (Matt. 20:28).

This is the exchange—the worthy Lord for unworthy sinners. He
has bought us. He has redeemed us. He has paid our debt and
we now do not belong to ourselves; we belong to Him who loved
us and gave Himself for us.

GOD'S PROVISION FOR SUBSTITUTION

In this world there is a universal law of substitution. Vicarious
suffering, substitution, a life for a life is a common concept in
everyday life and is one in which all of us share daily.

The Bible sometimes expresses it in poignant ways, such as
in the story of Abraham in Genesis 22. On Mount Moriah, in the
heart of Jerusalem, the site on which the temple was later built,
Abraham built an altar and laid his son Isaac upon it. When he
raised the dagger to plunge it into the heart of his boy, a voice
called from heaven, "Abraham, Abraham." The angel of the
Lord that stayed the plunging knife pointed to a ram caught in a
thicket. And Abraham offered the ram as a substitute for his son
Isaac. This is the law of substitution.

In Genesis 44, the eleven sons of Israel are seen standing
before the Egyptian prime minister who is the brother whom they
sold as a teenager into slavery. They did not recognize him; the
changing years had made him lord over Egypt. Finally, their
brother Joseph, still unknown to them, asked them to go back
and bring his full brother, Benjamin, who was born of his mother
Rachel. Then when he dismissed them to return to Canaan, he
said, "Benjamin must stay here with me."

There follows one of the most moving and dramatic of all the appeals you will read in human speech or literature. Judah went to the prime minister of Egypt and made appeal for his youngest brother, Benjamin. "How shall I go up to my father, and the lad be not with me?" (Gen. 44:34). The next verse reads, "Joseph could not refrain himself before all them that stood by him; and he cried . . ." (Gen. 45:1). When Judah said, "Take me as a substitute and let little Benjamin go back to his father lest we bring his old gray head down to the grave," Joseph could contain himself no longer, and he burst into tears. The tremendous dedication of Judah had broken his heart. "Take me and let my little brother go"—a priceless example of the law of substitution.

The whole sacrificial system was like that. The sinner came with his offering, with his sacrifice. Putting his hands over the victim, he confessed his sins, and the victim, a lamb or a bullock, was slain and the blood poured out before God.

Isaiah 53 shows this substitution:

> He was wounded for our transgressions, he was bruised for our iniquities: the chastisement of our peace was upon him; and with his stripes we are healed.
> All we like sheep have gone astray; we have turned every one to his own way; and the Lord hath laid on him the iniquity of us all (vv. 5–6).

That was the great fact of the gospel (*kerugma*) and the unequaled proclamation of the love of God in Christ Jesus. He took our place. He died in our stead. He was punished for our sins. He was made sin for us who knew no sin, that we might be received as righteous before God through His vicarious substitution.

It is a remarkable thing that Jesus did not come into this world like a Greek philosopher to discuss with us the things of the intellectual mind. Nor did men go out to hear just a prophet, the last and the greatest. Nor was He one who just stood and called men to the faith of Jehovah God. Rather, our Savior, the precious Jesus, came into the world to die for us. "In the [roll] of the book it is written of me. . . . Lo, I come to do thy will, O God" (Heb. 10:7, 9). And that will was that He die in our place. So much so that death is now robbed of its sting and the grave of its victory, and death to us is but the open door into heaven. We close our eyes on the heartaches, tears, sorrows, and hurts of this world, and we open our eyes upon the glories of heaven. Jesus has done this for us. And without fail, all of the apostles and witnesses have borne witness to that glorious gospel of the saving grace, the efficacious substitution that we know in Christ.

John the Baptist said,

> Behold the Lamb of God, which taketh away the sin of the world (John 1:29).

The beloved apostle John who leaned on the Lord's breast at the Lord's Table said:

> He is the propitiation for our sins: and not for ours only, but also for the sins of the whole world (1 John 2:2).

It is His blood that cleanseth us from all sins.

Peter may stumble in a thousand ways, but he does not stumble here.

> Who, when he was reviled, reviled not again; when he suffered, he threatened not; but committed himself to him that judgeth righteously:
> Who his own self bare our sins in his own body on the tree, that we, being dead to sins, should live unto righteousness: by whose stripes ye were healed (1 Pet. 2:23–24).

And consider the marvelous preaching of the apostle Paul:

> But God commendeth his love toward us, in that, while we were yet sinners, Christ died for us.
> For if, when we were enemies, we were reconciled to God by the death of his Son, much more, being reconciled, we shall be saved by his life (Rom. 5:8, 10).

And note the great moving introduction in the first chapter of the Revelation,

> And from Jesus Christ, who is the faithful witness, and the first begotten of the dead, and the prince of the kings of the earth. Unto him that loved us, and washed us from our sins in his own blood (1:5).

This is the gospel. This is what Jesus has done for us. He took our place and bore the judgment that should have fallen upon us, and in Him we have forgiveness of sins and an open door into heaven.

OUR SALVATION IS A GIFT

When we stand in the presence of the great throne of God on that sea of crystal glass, will our song be: "Look what I have done. I am here saved by my own merit. I have paid the debt. I have earned my salvation. It is something I won and achieved and do deserve"? Will that be our song? Or will it be: "I was a lost, dying, and condemned sinner, and He lifted me up out of the miry pit and set my feet on the rock. He forgave me my sins. He died in my stead, and my salvation is a gift from His gracious and loving hand. He did it for me."

That is the gospel! That is our praise now and forever! To Him who loved us and washed us from our sins in His own blood—to Him be glory and dominion forever and ever!

Think about those hosts of angels in heaven. In the Book of the Apocalypse we can read the hymns of praise that they offer unto Jesus. Standing on the golden floor of paradise, they address those beautiful words to our Lord Christ. He is the Captain of their host. He is the Crown Prince of Glory. He deserves the adoration and praise of the innumerable angels. How wonderful that will be! Oh, to be there someday and to listen to those angels by their uncounted myriads praise the Lord, the Prince of Glory!

But, an angel has never been blood-bought. An angel has never been redeemed. An angel has never been ransomed. No angel will ever have the experience we have—to die and to be buried and to be raised in resurrection glory. An angel has never known forgiveness of sin. Therefore, they can never sing as we can sing.

> E'er since by faith I saw the stream
>   Thy flowing wounds supply,
> Redeeming love has been my theme
>   And shall be till I die.
>
> When this poor lisping, stammering tongue
>   Lies silent in the grave,
> Then in a nobler, sweeter song
>   I'll sing Thy power to save.
>
> He saw me in my deep distress
>   And came to my relief,
> For me He bore the shameful cross
>   And carried all my grief.
>
> To Him I owe my life and breath
>   And all the joys I know;
> He makes me triumph over death
>   And saves me from the grave.

That shall be our song forever and ever.

15

How the Death of Christ Saves Us

> Forasmuch then as the children are partakers of flesh and blood, he also himself likewise took part of the same; that through death he might destroy him that had the power of death, that is, the devil;
> And deliver them who through fear of death were all their lifetime subject to bondage (Heb. 2:14–15).

In this chapter we confront what the Bible calls "the mystery of iniquity." It is referred to as "the mystery of God" in Revelation 10:7.

> But in the days of the voice of the seventh angel, when he shall begin to sound, the mystery of God should be finished, as he hath declared to his servants the prophets.

In 2 Thessalonians 2:7, Paul refers to it as the "mystery of iniquity."

> For the mystery of iniquity doth already work: only he who now letteth will let, until he be taken out of the way.

Why is it that God did not crush Satan during his rebellion in heaven? Why is it that God allowed Satan to destroy this beautiful and verdant earth? Why was he allowed to bathe it in human blood and to drown it in human tears? Violence, war, and suffering are on every page of its history, and its ultimate destiny is to be one of catastrophe. The earth is nothing other than a place in which to bury our dead. We cannot enter into that mystery of evil or the mystery of God. All we are able to do is just to look and to observe.

140

THE FEARFUL POWER OF SATAN

Satan is called a god. Paul refers to him as the god of this world (2 Cor. 4:4). He offered to Jesus the glory of all the nations of the earth, which belongs to him. Satan owns this world. He is awesome and fearful in himself. Even Michael, God's mighty warrior and archangel, dared not confront Satan.

> Yet Michael the archangel, when contending with the devil he disputed about the body of Moses, durst not bring against him a railing accusation, but said, The Lord rebuke thee (Jude 9).

Satan possesses awesome power in his own person.

He possesses fearful power in the demonic hosts that follow him. The angels of the hosts of heaven in the Revelation are numbered as ten thousand times ten thousand and thousands of thousands. The Greek reads *myriads* times *myriads* and *myriads* innumerable. Of that vast innumerable host, one third of the angels of heaven chose to follow Satan (Rev. 12:4). They are here in this earth—demons on every hand.

Satan is fearful and awesome in his kingdom. As there is a kingdom of light and life presided over by Christ the Lord, there is also a kingdom of darkness, death, and despair presided over by Satan, the prince of terrors. How else would you ever explain the thrust and march of communism, idolatry, and Islam, except it be energized by the power of Satan?

He is not only in himself a fearful and awesome person, but his ability to take every good thing in this earth and wreck it, throw it into havoc, damn it, and degrade is no less fearful than his personality. He takes everything good and adds sin to it and thus turns it into a curse. He takes love, the sweetest, tenderest of all feelings in the human heart, and adds sin to it, turning it into jealousy and inordinate concupiscence and promiscuity. He destroys it.

He takes the home, the dearest of all the memories of our childhood, and adds sin, and it becomes a place of misery, frustration, failure, tears, sorrow, and heartache. He takes money, one of the finest instruments that we possess to glorify God and through which we can send missionaries to Brazil and children to our church camp and with which we can magnify the cause of the Lord in building the Christian institutions of the land, but he adds sin and the love of money becomes as the Bible says, "The root of all evil." He takes everything good—movies, radio, television, the printing press—and damns them. These marvelous instruments of the media could glorify God and make the gospel known to the ends of the earth, but he adds sin to them, and they become instruments of violence, terror, and immorality. That is Satan. A car or a boat can be used for avocational happiness. But Satan adds sin, and they become instruments for desecrating the Lord's Day. Satan has the power to take everything good and destroy it.

The most fearsome and awesome power of Satan is seen in the way he can degrade and demean God's own people. Jesus said to Simon Barjona:

> Thou art Peter ["a rock," *petros*], and upon this rock I will build my church; and the gates of hell shall not prevail against it (Matt. 16:18).

Yet Satan took Simon Peter and wrapped him around his little finger. In the presence of a little maid, Simon Peter, named by Jesus "the rock," curses and swears, "I never knew Jesus! I never heard of Him!" Peter denies his own Lord. That is the power of Satan!

John, the beloved disciple, asks permission to bring fire down from heaven on those hated Samaritans (Luke 9:52–56). That is the power of Satan.

Simon Peter said to Ananias and Sapphira,

> Why hath Satan filled thine heart to lie to the Holy Ghost? (Acts 5:3).

That is the power of Satan.

In all the generations past his insidious presence has been a damning, destroying, degrading factor in human life. You would have thought that after the earth had been cleansed by the Flood, the earthly family beginning anew with God would be holy, separate, and apart. But shortly after Noah and his family came out of the ark, Ham found his father drunk and naked. Some scholars think that Ham then engaged in some aberrant sexual experience with his father. His family was consequently fearfully and awesomely cursed (Gen. 9:21–25).

You would have thought that when Israel came out of the fiery furnace and was delivered from Egypt, things would have been better. Instead, only two of their number ever entered the

Promised Land—Joshua and Caleb. The rest died under the curse of God in the wilderness.

The story of Israel in the Promised Land during the days of the judges is one repetitive sentence after another, "And the children of Israel did evil in the sight of the LORD" and God delivered them into the hands of their enemies.

You would think that Israel would do better under the kings. Saul, their first king, was eaten up with jealousy, and the Spirit of the Lord departed from him. David brought reproach on the name of God forever. Solomon with his seven hundred wives and three hundred concubines brought Israel down to the pit of sin.

You would have thought that in the purging fires of the Babylonian captivity things would be better. Instead, the nation descended to its lowest depth and finally was destroyed as a nation in A.D. 70.

If this is the power of Satan with God's own chosen people, what shall we do but stand in terrified awe at the history of the nations beyond the realm and the chosen elective purposes of God! How could you ever describe in mere speech the sorrow, ravages, heartache, and bloodletting of a Genghis Khan, a Tamerlane, or an Adolph Hitler. The whole earth was bathed in sorrow, tears, and blood. This is the world and the kingdom and the power of Satan.

CHRIST CAME TO BREAK IT UP

The text says that our Lord came into the world to break up the kingdom of Satan. He came to deliver us from the power of death and from him who has it, namely, Satan—the devil, Lucifer, the fallen archangel of God.

As I read the Scriptures, I am constantly confirmed in my persuasion that Satan thought he had the kingdom forever. He believed that sin with its judgment and death would reign forever. He believed that he would be king of terrors forever.

When Jesus was crucified and died on the tree, how Satan must have exulted! Israel, the promised people, had slain her own son. Look at Him! He is dead, nailed to a cross! The promises of God are fallen down to the ground and into the dust. Sin, death, the grave, violence, and blasphemy will live forever, and he—Satan—is king over it all!

But there was a great mystery (*musterion*), a great secret kept in the heart of God that Satan did not know. In the descent of Christ our Lord into human flesh, and finally through death into the grave, He grappled with the king of sin and death and came out triumphant. He became flesh like us. We, the children, are made out of flesh and blood. He was made like us. And being in the flesh, He became subject unto death that through death He might destroy him who had the power of death, namely, Satan.

We now enter a world that is barely exhibited in the Bible. During the three days following Jesus' death—Friday, Saturday, and Sunday—He went down into hades (*sheol*), and there He confronted Satan—the devil or Lucifer—and the spirits of darkness.

We have a hint of it in 1 Peter 3. Peter says the Lord went down into the grave, and into that silent earth He proclaimed the gospel of deliverance and victory.

> For Christ also hath once suffered for sins, the just for the unjust, that he might bring us to God, being put to death in the flesh, but quickened by the Spirit:
> By which also he went and preached unto the spirits in prison;
> Which sometime were disobedient (vv. 18–20a).

In Ephesians 4, the Lord is described as entering into heaven taking captivity captive, entering into glory with all of the delivered Old Testament saints. As in a great Roman triumph, our Lord entered into heaven victorious over sin, death, and the grave! This He did for us when He became man and died and entered the grave.

But there is more. In His resurrection He opened the door for the rest of us. Paul could write in such victorious triumph:

> O death, where is thy sting? [He has taken it away.] O grave, where is thy victory? [Christ has taken it away.] (1 Cor. 15:55).

We now are victorious, whereas we once lived in defeat.

But there is still more. The greatest, the finest, the best of all that Christ has done for us in the pouring out of the crimson of His life is something that you and I experience.

> For if, when we were enemies, we were reconciled to God by the death of his Son, much more, being reconciled, we shall be saved by his life (Rom. 5:10).

144

We are saved by His resurrected, regenerating life, by the power of Christ to enter our human hearts, lives, homes, and world in order to remake, regenerate, and recreate.

When I speak of the Lord descending into the depths of the nether world, my mind can hardly encompass it. I read in the Scriptures and behold in wonder the mystery. But when it speaks of Christ saving us by His life, then we enter the realm of human experience, and I can verify its marvelous truth.

What is the meaning for us when the Lord Christ died on the cross and poured out the crimson of His life into the life stream of humanity? Is there power in the death and resurrection of Jesus? Is there ability in Him to regenerate, to recreate, to make anew, to save?

It is a wonderful thing—the pouring out of the life of our Lord into this earth! I think of the marvelous First Baptist Church in Dallas. Dr. Truett, my predecessor, stood behind the sacred pulpit desk in Dallas for forty-seven years. He died while still pastor of the church, having poured his life into this congregation for all those years. I inherited from his gracious hand and marvelous ministry blessings untold, unspeakable, indescribable.

From our forefathers who wrote the Constitution, declared themselves independent, and sealed their commitment to liberty with their own lives and sacred fortunes, we today have inherited blessings unspeakable—the right to meet together, to preach the gospel, to work and to advance as far as each one of us may have talent or ability to achieve. The freedoms of America are a gift from the forefathers who lived before us.

My own parents poured their very lives into me. How could I ever thank them enough for the sacrifices they made for me?

This is but a small approach, a limited illustration of those vast, immeasurable blessings poured into this earth in the crimson life and blood of Jesus Christ our Lord. I stand amazed in the presence of Jesus the Nazarene.

The world plays, like a ploy, with the manifestations of sin but never grapples with its causes. Secular reform just plays with the outward appearances of sin. It is as an ungifted doctor, unaware of his assignment, would play with the pimples on the skin when the cause of the disease is in the bloodstream. The ploys of secular reformational movements are so superficial. By law, you can take the gun from the hand of the murderer, but in his heart he is still a murderer. By law, you can take the needle from the dope addict, but in his heart he is still a dope addict. By law, you can take the bottle away from the drunkard, but in his heart he is still a drunkard. You can take the harlot away from her paramour, but in her heart she is still a prostitute. Our penitentiaries, jails, reformatories, and policemen are but monuments to the failure of social and secular reforms.

Jesus, through His life and in the pouring out of His blood, brought to us not merely a new suit, but the creation of a new man, the making of a new people, a regenerated generation. The power of the poured out life of Christ makes us anew!

There is not a pastor in the world whose heart is not full of marvelous memories and illustrations of the power of Christ to save, to regenerate, to make anew. A book was placed in my hand, the title of which intrigued me. It is entitled *Unshackled*. It is a book recounting the modern miracles of regeneration in the Pacific Garden Mission in Chicago. I was especially sensitive to it since I once visited that mission. When I was a youth, meandering one night down the streets of Chicago, I heard Christian singing. I soon found myself in the Pacific Garden Mission. If I were to live a thousand years, I could never forget that service. The worshipers there were out of the gutter, out of the bawdy house, out of the depths of sin, but they were new people. The drunkard had lifted up his head in honor. The harlot was there sanctified, purified, and cleansed. The prodigal son was there preparing to go back to his father's home. That man out of the gutter was there with the crown of sainthood on his brow. They sang, they testified, they glorified the Lord, they witnessed to the saving grace of Christ in them. What an impression it made upon me as a youth!

But I have seen it again and again. Down the aisle of our great church have come men from that stream of life that goes through the YMCA, which is located directly across the street from our church. They are men who have been marvelously rescued by the loving grace and power of the regenerating presence of Jesus. That is a miracle!

But there is yet another great miracle. It is you. However marvelous it may be to see a man lifted up out of the depths of the sewer or a woman raised up out of a house of harlotry, it is more wonderful to see lives that have never known the debauchery and the abysmal damnation that sin can bring into the human life. It is more wonderful to see children, teenagers, young couples, and families that stand strong and pure in the presence of the great God our Savior, Christ Jesus. That is the greatest of all.

That is the life you and I have known through our church, through our Christian parents. When we were saved, when the Lord touched our hearts and led us to that humble commitment to the blessed Jesus, we were saved by the blood, the death, the Resurrection, and the life of the "crucified One."

> Saved by the blood of the Crucified One!
> All praise to the Father, all praise to the Son,
> All praise to the Spirit, the great Three in One!
> Saved by the blood of the Crucified One!

16

Our Lord's Entrance Into the Grave

> But we see Jesus, who was made a little lower than the angels for the suffering of death, crowned with glory and honor; that he by the grace of God should taste death for every man.
>
> Forasmuch then as the children are partakers of flesh and blood, he also himself likewise took part of the same; that through death he might destroy him that had the power of death, that is, the devil;
>
> And deliver them who through fear of death were all their lifetime subject to bondage (Heb. 2:9, 14–15).

The Dread of Death Is Common to All Mankind

There is no more common denominator to all mankind than the horror, terror, and dread we fear before death. When death reaches forth her cold and clammy hands to lay hold upon us and when we view the immediate prospect of the decay and the corruption of our body, we join mankind who through the centuries has always felt the horror and the terror of death. In the ancient world, death was pictured as a pitiless divinity. In our modern day, death is pictured as a grim reaper with a scythe or in the likeness of a skull and crossbones. In the Old Testament Scriptures, death is called the "kings of terrors" (Job 18:14). In Psalm 55, the psalmist cries before "the terrors of death" that are beginning to fall upon him.

In the New Testament the red horse of war and slaughter is followed by the black horse of famine and want, and finally all are followed by the pale horse whose rider is death and whose follower is the grave (Rev. 6).

In the Metropolitan Art Museum in New York, I saw a painting entitled "The Race of Death." On an oblong race track there is a man riding a fleet animal, but immediately behind him, pursuing him and gaining on him, is another rider. The rider on that horse is a skeleton—death.

All of the love in our hearts for anyone in our beloved circle of family is not able to cover over or hide the awesome visage of death. Abraham said to the sons of Heth, "give me a possession of a burying place with you, that I may bury my dead out of my sight" (Gen. 23:4). He was speaking of his beloved Sarah.

All of the honor and glory of the world cannot hide the fearsome face of the specter of death. Military tribunals, citations, medals, plaudits, and all of the accolades of the human heart cannot change that terrible reality—death.

As many of you have done, I have stood in the Arlington National Cemetery across the Potomac from our nation's capitol and watched representatives from our armed forces march back and forth in front of the Tomb of the Unknown Soldier. And the soldier speaks:

> Listen, youngster, you who thrill so
> To the sound of marching feet,
> To the call of bugles blending
> With the drum's rhythmatic beat;
> Listen to those bands a-playing,
> 'Neath your country's flag a-flying,
> But listen, youngster, I am praying;
> There is no glory in your dying.
>
> Listen, youngster, you who love so
> All the glamour of parade;
> Buttons do not shine so brightly
> When you're standing, sick, afraid,
> In the thick of war's inferno,
> When your flag is drenched with blood,
> Blood of comrades, swaying, praying,
> Knee deep in a trench of mud.
>
> Listen, youngster, bands cease playing
> In the hell-fire of the fight;
> Screaming shells will be your music,
> Singing hymns of death and fright;
> Shells that kill or make you beggars,

Legless on some city street;
Men with tin cups in a doorway—
Ask them, son, if war is sweet.

Here I lie, The Unknown Soldier,
Wreaths of nations line my bed,
Honors have been heaped upon me,
But listen, youngster, I AM DEAD!
Somewhere in this land you love so,
Someone's waiting for me still,
Wonders could I be their loved one,
Forever wonders, ever will.

Listen, youngster, you who thrill so
When plumes and bayonets sparkle bright,
There is no beauty in death's plumage—
Only bones bleached bare and white.
Listen, youngster, you want glory—
I've had glory, honors spread
Above my tomb in countless numbers,
But listen, youngster, I AM DEAD:

All of the honor, glory, tributes, plaudits, and accolades of human speech cannot hide the awesome visage of death.

THAT TERRIBLE DREAD IN THE LIFE OF JESUS

That dread and terror of death was doubly heightened in the life of our Lord.

> Now is my soul troubled; and what shall I say? Father, save me from this hour: but for this cause came I unto this hour (John 12:27).

In the Garden of Gethsemane there is a poignant description of our Savior's dread before His death. In an agony in which the pouring of the perspiration from His brow was like blood dropping to the ground, He asked,

> Father, if thou be willing, remove this cup from me: nevertheless not my will, but thine, be done (Luke 22:42).

Why did our Lord have such a dread of death? One reason was that His death was voluntary. It was not coerced. He volunteered in heaven before the foundation of the world. In Hebrews 10, He is depicted as standing before God, offering His life as an atonement for our sins.

> Wherefore when he cometh into the world, he saith, Sacrifice and offering thou wouldest not, but a body hast thou prepared me:

> Then said I, Lo, I come (in the volume of the book it is written of me,) to do thy will, O God (Heb. 10:5, 7).

The Lord Jesus said of His coming death:

> Even as the Son of man came not to be ministered unto, but to minister, and to give his life a ransom for many (Matt. 20:28).

> No man taketh it from me, but I lay it down of myself. I have power to lay it down, and I have power to take it again. This commandment have I received of my Father (John 10:18).

It was a voluntary assignment accepted on the part of our Savior. We *have* to die. There is no choice with us. "The wages of sin is death. . . ." (Rom. 6:23). We have sinned, and we face the inevitable judgment of God. The curse of death is written on every member of our physical frame. But our Lord was not bound by that curse. Because He was sinless, death had no hold upon Him. He was free of sin and the judgment and penalty it entails. Our Lord accepted the assignment of death in our behalf, for our cause. He gave Himself willingly. There were 72,000 angels—twelve legions—who were straining to deliver Him, yet He refused their presence. When He suffered on the cross, kind people gave to our Lord a mixture of sour wine and myrrh, a narcotic to deaden His senses. He refused to drink it. Our Lord faced death in clarity of mind with full and unabated consciousness. It was a voluntary act on His part. He accepted the assignment and died.

There is a second reason for our Lord's dread in facing death. Man has never invented a death so cruel as crucifixion. In an encyclopedia article that I read on crucifixion, there is one sentence that stayed in my mind. "Crucifixion by death is not to die one time, but a thousand times." So vile and terrible was death by crucifixion that the Roman government prohibited this method from ever being used against a Roman citizen. Death by crucifixion was reserved for alien slaves and criminals.

A third reason for our Lord's dread before death concerns the mystery of God.

> Yet it pleased the LORD to bruise him; he hath put him to grief: when thou shalt make his soul an offering for sin, he shall see his seed, he shall prolong his days, and the pleasure of the Lord shall prosper in his hand.

> He shall see of the travail of his soul, and shall be satisfied (Is. 53:10–11b).

I cannot enter into that. So deep is the mystery of the agony of our Lord in His death that the sun refused to shine and darkness hid it from sight. From 12:00 high noon until 3:00 in the afternoon, the whole earth was darkened as Jesus suffered and died. He bore the curse, the penalty, the judgment of sin for all humanity. I cannot enter into it. Even God shut it out.

> Well might the sun in darkness hide
> And shut His glories in,
> When Christ, the mighty Maker died
> For man the creature's sin.

THE DESCRIPTIVE TEXT

In the presentation of the death of our Lord in our text in Hebrews, there are some words that describe the agony and the travail of that Atonement.

> But we see Jesus, who was made a little lower than the angels for the suffering of death, crowned with glory and honor; that he by the grace of God should taste death for every man (Heb. 2:9).

In the English translation, "for every man" is last. In the Greek text, that phrase is first. The emphatic word in the clause is "instead of," "in behalf of," "for the sake of," "in place of" (*huper*) every man.

That the Lord was crucified was not a unique event in the history of the Roman empire. The Romans crucified hundreds of thousands of their enemies. Spartacus the gladiator, in his rebellion, gathered one hundred thousand gladiatorial combatant slaves around him, and it is an amazing thing to me to read in history that they fought the Roman legions for three years. When the Roman legions finally won that bitter and awesome confrontation, they crucified six thousand of those gladiators along the Appian Way next to the city. Our Lord was not unique in that He was crucified. The uniqueness of the death of our Lord is that He died (*huper*) "instead of," "in the place of" each one of us. No other man ever did that or ever shall do that but Jesus. Upon Him was our curse, and all of the judgment of God that should have been ours was heaped upon him. He died in our stead. He paid the penalty for our sins.

Note another thought the author presents about the death of Christ. "He by the grace of God should *taste* death for every man." "Taste death"' is a Hebraism of a way the Hebrews spoke. The Greek word *geuomai* means "to taste," but when you place it with *thanatos,* meaning "death," it refers to the deep experience of all that death contains. He should taste death—not a brief, temporary experience—but in that cup was all that death means, and He drank it to the last dregs. He emptied the cup.

What a remarkable thing is the gospel of the cross. No wonder Paul said, "God forbid that I should glory, save in the cross of our Lord Jesus Christ" (Gal. 6:14). No wonder they place the cross on the top of our churches. It is a sign, an aegis of the Christian faith—*In Hoc Signo Vinces,* "By This Sign Conquer"—the sign of the cross.

The cross is an exhibition of the depravity of the human race. If you want to see what mankind is like, look at the crucifixion of Jesus. But it is also a sign of the mercy and grace of God that He was crucified. He died in our behalf. God so loved us that He gave His Son to the cruel cross. That is an unbelievable mercy of God, for out of the cross flows all of the grace, hope, and salvation from our sin. Christ did on the cross what we could never do; namely, He brought salvation and victory over sin out of suffering and death.

When a man dies, he dies for himself. There are no streams of grace and forgiveness that flow out of the death of a George Washington, a Zoroaster, a Mahavira a Gautama Buddha, or an Islamic Muhammad. These men died. They died for themselves. We die, and we also die for ourselves. But out of the death of our Lord flow those streams of mercy and grace that bring to us forgiveness of sin and new hope and a new life. It is a mystery of God that by the grace of the great, mighty God, He should taste death, experience death for every one of us. It is a wonder.

THE GREAT COMPASSIONATE SAVIOR

But that is not all. In the death of our Lord He identified Himself with us and became our great compassionate Savior. Look at the consummation of the age, at the end of human history. All the nations of the world are to be gathered before the great and mighty Lord who sits upon the throne of His glory. In Matthew 25, we see our Lord seated as the Judge of all the earth, and we and all humanity are gathered before Him. And when that day comes, there is a sullen bitterness expressed on the part of all who are being judged. They shake their fists at the almighty omnipotent Judge and say: "How can You judge us? You live in heaven where all is sweetness and light and glory and happiness and bliss. But we live in this darkened world of tears, sorrow, heartache, and death! How can You judge us? What do You know about us?"

As they declaim against the Lord on His throne, a woman with dark hair and dark eyes and olive skin pulls back her sleeve and says to the Judge of all the earth: "Do You see this number tatooed on my arm? I was raped, beaten, tortured, and killed in a Nazi concentration camp! What do You know about that?"

A black man rolls down his collar and says to the Judge of all the earth: "Do You see that? I was lynched just because I was black. Do You see that?"

And another stands before the Judge of all the earth and says: "I was exiled in a Siberian slave camp, and I knew hunger and thirst all the days of my life. What do You know about that?"

Another one comes before the Judge and says: "I was executed, though innocent, and I died! The cruel hands of the law seized me, and I was innocent! Do You know that?"

And as that great throng speaks before the Judge of all the earth, they say, "Whoever judges us ought to be one of us, ought to understand us, ought to know us, ought to live our lives. Whoever judges us ought to be born a Jew in a hated and despised country like Nazi Germany. He ought to be born illegitimate where they say, 'We do not even know the name of his father.' Whoever judges us ought to be someone who was born poor and who knew nothing but want and hunger all of his life. Whoever judges us ought to be one who was denied by his own people and rejected by his own nation. Whoever judges us ought to be one who is despised and rejected of men and who is betrayed by his own friends. Whoever judges us ought to be one who was executed between thieves and felons and criminals."

While they are speaking, a great silence and hush falls over the vast throng before the King of glory. Unknowingly, they have described Him! They have been speaking of Him, the Great Judge of all the earth. He was born into a hated and outcast family. He was born poor, born to suffer, born to be rejected, born in grief and sorrow, born and executed like a criminal. And that is why the author of Hebrews says,

154

> For verily he took not on him the nature of angels; but he took on him the seed of Abraham.
>
> Wherefore in all things it behooved him to be made like unto his brethren, that he might be a merciful and faithful high priest in things pertaining to God, to make reconciliation for the sins of the people.
>
> For in that he himself hath suffered being tempted, he is able to succor them that are tempted (Heb. 2:16–18).

That is why we have this beautiful invitation in Hebrews 4:

> Seeing then that we have a great high priest, that is passed into the heavens, Jesus the Son of God let us hold fast our profession.
>
> For we have not an high priest which cannot be touched with the feeling of our infirmities; but was in all points tempted like as we are, yet without sin.
>
> Let us therefore come boldly unto the throne of grace, that we may obtain mercy, and find grace to help in time of need (vv. 14–16).

He knows all about us. There is no one who has suffered, but that He has suffered. No one has cried, but that He has wept bitter tears. No one has felt alone and forsaken, but that He was alone and forsaken. No one has died, but that He died. Therefore, come boldly to the throne of grace. Oh, what a Savior! What a friend! What a great intercessor! What a mediator! What a representative! What a great God—our blessed Lord Jesus!

17

Our Lord's Entrance Into Resurrection Life

> And the angel answered and said unto the women, Fear not ye: for I know that ye seek Jesus, which was crucified.
> He is not here: for he is risen, as he said. Come, see the place where the Lord lay (Matt. 28:5–6).

Many years ago I listened to a wonderful missionary from China, Dr. E. M. Poteat. He described a scene that I so well remember. He was lecturing to his class at the University of Shanghai on the resurrection of our Lord. One of the students spoke up and said, "Sir, I do not believe that." Dr. Poteat asked the young man, "Why?" The student replied, "Sir, dead men do not rise again."

All of the dead whom I have ever seen or of whom I have ever heard are still dead, and apparently they stay dead forever. I can understand the feeling of that young college student. I never saw a dead man rise again. What makes you think that there might be an escape? What makes you think that Jesus was an exception, that He was raised from among the dead, and that He lives? Is it possible that if somebody escaped, then maybe ultimately all of us can? I must have an answer, for it is basic for every hope we entertain in our hearts. Did Christ rise from the dead? Is it false or is it fact? Every hope that we hold dear to our souls is dependent upon the truth of that answer.

There are some things that happen in history that are debatable. The historians discuss them back and forth. Whether they are true or not has no particular significance; the historians just debate them. Did Alexander the Great, when he came to the Indus River, weep because there were no more worlds to conquer? It does not matter one way or the other. It is just something that the historians can discuss. Did Caesar cross the Rubican? It does not matter. It is just a discussion debated in history. Did Washington throw a dollar across the Delaware River? Did he chop down the famous cherry tree? It does not matter. It is just a discussion in history. But it is all significant, all consequential, and it deeply matters whether or not it is fact that Jesus was raised from among the dead.

In Matthew 28:17, there is a strange phrase. The scene is an appointed mountain in Galilee where Jesus appeared before more than five hundred brethren at once.

> And when they saw him, they worshiped him: *but some doubted.*

He is standing there, resurrected, immortalized, glorified in their presence, and then there is the strangest little clause, "but some doubted." There is something that God has to do to affirm and to communicate truth to our hearts. Otherwise it never becomes factual or true.

You have a brilliant instance of that in the history of Dallas. Did Lee Harvey Oswald assassinate John Fitzgerald Kennedy unaided, unassisted, and without conspiracy? You can ask the American people if they believe the Warren Commission report concerning the assassination, and half of them will say yes, and half of them will say no. After his survey of American opinion, George Gallup, the famous pollster, replied, "Fifty per cent believed the report and fifty per cent did not believe it." There has never been an incident in history so thoroughly investigated as the assassination of President Kennedy, nor has there been an investigation so immediately following the tragedy. In the last congressional session, millions of dollars were appropriated for that further meticulous interrogation, and still the American people are divided in their belief as to whether or not there was a conspiracy.

There has to be something from God to affirm the truth in our hearts. Luke, the historian, avowed that he carefully went through all of the evidence about the life of our Lord and wrote it down. This is the third gospel. Can I believe that? Is that fact and truth for me? It lies in the affirmation of God. All I can do is to present the undeniable, unassailable, incontrovertible facts of the resurrection of our Lord, but its truth and power lie in the affirmation of the Spirit of God in your heart. Here are the facts.

A Philosophical Fact

There has never been a life so beautiful, so tender, so humble, so self-effacing, so given to ministry as the life of our Lord, preaching the gospel to the poor, healing the sick, blessing the people. His words were as none that had ever been spoken before. Those who listened to Him said, "Never a man spake like that man." You can read them for yourself. They are incomparable. As the people watched Him in His acts and ministries, they said, "It was never so seen in Israel." There was never a life like our Lord. Yet it ended in ignominy, shame, and crucifixion.

That posits an insoluble mystery. How could a life so beautiful, so preciously dear, so tenderly meaningful in ministry end in such tragedy, evil, and shame? Will evil forever triumph over good? Will wrong forever triumph over right? Will death, terror, violence, and wrong reign forever? Is there not another chapter? Is there not another story, another ending? Is there not some way that human life comes into triumph, glory, and goodness, without finding itself buried in the grave of wrong and death and sin? Is there not some answer to that insoluble, impenetrable, dark mystery—the end of life?

A Pragmatic, Empirical Fact

Concerning the life of our Lord, we must face an empirical, practical fact: What became of His body? On Friday, He was embalmed, wrapped with a hundred pounds of spices, laid in a tomb that was sealed and guarded by a Roman contingency. Sunday, the grave clothes were beautifully undisturbed, but He was gone. What happened? How do you account for it?

Within days, Simon Peter was standing with the other apostles proclaiming to the world that Jesus had been raised from among the dead and that He lived! For the Sadducees, who did not believe in the resurrection of the dead, or for the Roman soldiers who had crucified Him and were supposed to guard Him, all it would have taken to silence Simon Peter forever was to produce the decaying, dead body of our Lord. Yet they did not do it. Why? Because they did not have it. Something had happened, and the body had disappeared.

There are two alternatives: either human hands had taken the body away, or supernatural hands had taken it away. If human hands had taken it away, then it was done by either His friends or His foes. His friends could not have taken the body away. They were not capable. The tomb was closed with a Roman seal, and the Roman soldiers stood there to guard it. Had they stolen the body surreptitiously and furtively, how was it that the grave clothes were so undisturbed?

Did His foes steal His body away? That was the exact thing they were there to prevent. They did not want anyone to steal His body away and then say that He was raised from the dead. It is a plain, empirical, practical fact that the body of Jesus was gone. The tomb was empty.

A PSYCHOLOGICAL FACT

There is another fact about our Lord. It is this: the marvelous, wonderful transformation of the apostles is a psychological fact. When they saw Jesus die on Friday, they were plunged into abysmal, indescribable despair and agony. The Roman centurion officially reported to Pilate, "He is dead." Pilate, the Roman procurator, marveled that He had died so soon, so to make doubly sure a Roman soldier took a spear and thrust it into Jesus' heart, and out of His side poured the crimson of His life. The Sadducees looked upon Him and saw that He was dead. The Pharisees congratulated themselves saying, "He is dead." The passersby looked and said, "He is dead." The women came to the tomb to embalm a dead body. When He appeared to the apostles, they thought they had seen an apparition. Thomas, one of the apostles, said, "Except I . . . put my finger into the print of the nails, and thrust my hand into his side, I will not believe" (John 20:25).

Then suddenly the whole world was livid with the spontaneous cries, "He is alive!" "I have seen Him!" said Mary Magdalene. "I have seen Him!" said Simon Peter. "We have seen Him!" exclaimed the eleven. "We have seen Him!" said the five hundred brethren. And for forty days He appeared to first one and then another. What happened?

159

Some skeptics will explain away what happened. They suggest that those apostles gathered together in some secret place and said: "This is horrible. Let us pretend that He is alive. Let us say that He arose from the dead." Then those who believe in Him go out and lay down their lives for a lie! They are persecuted unto death. Some of them are thrown into boiling caldrons of oil; some of them are burned at the stake; some of them are crucified for a known lie! It is psychologically impossible! They sealed their testimony with their blood, for they had seen Him raised from among the dead! Jesus lives! He is alive! It is a psychological fact.

AN ECCLESIASTICAL FACT

But there is still another fact concerning our Lord. The church is an ecclesiastical fact. There are churches all over the earth. From where did the church come? It was formed by the Jews, and the first members were Jews. In Acts 2 we read that 3,000 of them were baptized at one time. Acts 4 testifies that 5,000 men, not counting the women, were baptized. Acts 6 says that there were great multitudes of the priests who were obedient to the faith. Continue through the Book of Acts, and you will find that the multitudes are too great to be counted.

A historian has suggested that there were between 50,000 and 100,000 belonging to that first church in Jerusalem. How do you explain that? Deuteronomy 21:23 expressly says, "For he that is hanged is accursed of God." Do you mean to tell me that those Jewish people look back to a dead, crucified malefactor for their Lord and for the organization of the church? No. The church began in a gloriously, heraldic announcement, "Jesus is alive!"

That little band of common people, mostly slaves, faced the entire system of state worship in the Graeco-Roman empire and challenged it to the death. The Roman Caesar made his presence and his image and his idol part of the national worship. To deny worship to the Roman Caesar was to be traitorous to the Roman empire and thus an enemy of the state and of the emperor. The people paid for their faith in Christ in death. They were literally baptized in blood and burned in fire! How do you account for the church? It lives today. In the Communist world there is an underground church; its members serve in slave camps, but the church lives! Where did it come from? It is an ecclesiastical fact.

A Soteriological Fact

We yet consider another fact concerning our Lord. It is a soteriological fact. It is seen in the marvelous conversion and transformation of Saul of Tarsus, who became Paul the apostle. What a mighty man he was! What a mighty mind he possessed! Thirteen of the letters in the New Testament are from the apostle Paul. Also, the Book of Hebrews is completely Pauline. His dear friend and physician, Dr. Luke, wrote the Books of Luke and Acts. That means the apostle Paul wrote or heavily influenced sixteen books out of the twenty-seven in the New Testament. They are the works of a marvelous and wonderful mind.

From where did Paul come? He thought that he was doing God's will to persecute the church unto the death. Having received letters from the high priest, he was going to Damascus to hail into prison and execution those who called upon the name of the Lord Jesus. But on the way he said, "I saw the risen and resurrected Lord." He wrote in 1 Corinthians:

> For I delivered unto you first of all that which I also received, how that Christ died for our sins according to the scriptures;
>
> And that he was buried, and that he rose again the third day according to the scriptures:
>
> And that he was seen of Cephas, then of the twelve:
>
> After that, he was seen of above five hundred brethren at once; of whom the greater part remain unto this present, but some are fallen asleep.
>
> After that, he was seen of James; then of all the apostles.
>
> And last of all he was seen of me also, as of one born out of due time [before Israel sees her Lord Messiah and is converted in a day] (15:3–8).

When the Lord appeared to Paul, he was wonderfully saved. That was in a day when every fact and every evidence could be carefully checked and verified. If the apostle Paul made a false statement, there were those who were capable of denying it. A marvelous soteriological fact is found in the incomparably meaningful transformation and conversion of the apostle Paul. Paul said, "I have seen Him with my own eyes, heard Him with my own ears. He is alive!"

A Literary Fact

Concerning the Lord we must yet consider another fact. We have here in the blessed Book four gospels about the life of our

Lord—incomparable pieces of literature. Those gospels achieve an assignment that is impossible to the greatest geniuses of literature who ever lived: namely, how do you record as though it were beautifully normal, the conversing of God with man? How do you do it? To achieve that has been the despair and failure of the most magnificently gifted writers the world has seen.

Look at it for yourself. The gods of Homer are manifestly fictitious. The story of the *Iliad* and the *Odyssey* is fiction. It sounds like it. It reads like it. Look at the writing of the greatest genius of all time—the myriad-minded Shakespeare. His writing of the ghost that speaks in *Hamlet* is manifestly and patently the effort of a laborious imagination. It is fiction. You sense it when you read that greatest of all dramatic tragedies. But then read Matthew 28, Luke 24, Mark 16, John 20 and 21. Innately, internally, inherently, deep in it is the sense of the recounting of a beautiful and precious truth—the risen Christ in conversation with men. It is normal, beautiful, real, and factual because it happened. It is truth—a literary fact. Look at it for yourself.

An Experiential Fact

But there is one other incontrovertible fact. The fact that He is alive can be verified and affirmed in our hearts and lives. Alexander the Great is dead. Caesars Julius and Augustus are dead. Charlemagne is dead. William the Conqueror is dead. Washington is dead. Churchill is dead. It would never occur to one of us to bow in the presence of any of these great men of the past and pray and beseech their favor and blessing. They are dead. But the smallest child can be taught to kneel and to pray to the Lord Jesus. The experience is beautifully natural and spiritually moving. Even the child will answer normally. How much more for us who have been taught in the faith in the decades of the passing years to talk to the Lord Jesus who is alive, who bows down His ear from heaven to hear, and who helps us in our pilgrim way! He is alive. He lives. It is an experiential fact.

On a plane a man approached me and said, "Are you W. A. Criswell?" I said, "Yes." He sat down by my side, and as the time passed he began to talk about himself. He was a graduate of one of the world-famous liberal seminaries in America. Having been taught in the liberal seminary, he was introduced to all of those academic theories concerning the Word of God, such as

162

the documentary hypothesis, which concludes that the Scripture is a fabric of forgery and fakery, denying the supernatural, the miracles, and the Resurrection. His degree was from that learned institution. After he was graduated, he became the associate pastor of a world-famous church, the largest of his denomination. He said, "I walked in and among the people in my unbelief, infidelity, and in my denial of the faith."

That is a strange thing. The real enemies of God are not out there somewhere; they are in the church. The man continued: "One day in a communion service, as I was taking the broken bread and drinking the fruit of the vine, I had a marvelous experience. I cannot describe it. I began to realize that Jesus died for my sins in order that I might be saved. There came upon me a tremendous realization that Jesus was raised bodily from the dead and that He lives! My Savior lives!"

As he recounted his own experience, I could not help but think of John Wesley who, as a minister, was listening to another minister reading *The Introduction to the Book of Romans* by Martin Luther, and wrote in his journal, "I felt my heart strangely warmed." John Wesley went out and became a flame of fire preaching the gospel of the Son of God. As I listened to that young man, I remembered that experience in Wesley's life.

The young man continued: "I turned from that service with Christ in my heart. I resigned my place as the associate pastor of that liberal church. I am now preaching in a school house, and I have gathered together a little band of believers. Every day I go from door to door witnessing to the people of the grace of our Lord in Christ Jesus. He is my Savior, and He has saved me." He paused and looked at me with searching, penetrating eyes and said, "Would you ever have thought that I would be knocking at a door, telling people about Jesus!"

That is an experiential fact. What that man has experienced, ten thousand others of us would say: "Amen. Glory to God! That is right! He lives! I know He lives! He walks by my side. He helps me in my hour of need. I trust Him as my Savior. Someday I look forward to seeing Him face to face."

What a gospel! What a truth! What a fact! It is indisputable, unassailable, undeniable, forever affirmed—He is alive!

18

The Great Fact of the Gospel:
Jesus Is Alive

And as they thus spake, Jesus himself stood in the midst of them, and saith unto them, Peace be unto you.

But they were terrified and affrighted, and supposed that they had seen a spirit.

And he said unto them, Why are ye troubled? and why to thoughts arise in your hearts?

Behold my hands and my feet, that it is I myself: handle me, and see; for a spirit hath not flesh and bones, as ye see me have.

And when he had thus spoken, he showed them his hands and his feet.

And while they yet believed not for joy, and wondered, he said unto them, Have ye here any meat?

And they gave him a piece of a broiled fish, and of an honeycomb.

And he took it, and did eat before them (Luke 24:36–43).

And if Christ be not raised, your faith is vain; ye are yet in your sins.

Then they also which are fallen asleep in Christ are perished.

If in this life only we have hope in Christ, we are of all men most miserable.

But now is Christ risen from the dead, and become the first fruits of them that slept (1 Cor. 15:17–20).

The central, cardinal fact of the gospel, not the primary premise, supposition, or hypothetical metaphysical theory, but the great reality and central fact of the gospel is this: "Jesus is alive."

They Recognized "This Same Jesus"

It is a remarkable thing that the emphasis of the Scriptures upon the risen Lord is that He is this same Jesus. They use those words "this same Jesus." But as gloriously remarkable as it is that He who was crucified and buried is alive—it is no less remarkable that the same human recognitions that characterized Him in the days of His flesh characterize Him now. Little personality traits, the human idiosyncrasies, those things that make one distinctive and unique, Jesus possessed them in His life, and after being raised from the dead, He still possessed them. He was no different.

Note the account of the race of Simon Peter and John to the tomb after Mary Magdalene had come and said, "The tomb is empty!"

> So they ran both together: and the other disciple [John] did outrun Peter, and came first to the sepulcher.
> And he stooping down, and looking in, saw the linen clothes lying; yet went he not in.
> Then cometh Simon Peter following him, and went into the sepulcher, and seeth the linen clothes lie,
> And the napkin, that was about his head, not lying with the linen clothes, but wrapped together in a place by itself.
> Then went in also that other disciple, which came first to the sepulcher, and he saw, and believed (John 20:4–8).

John recognized the way that Jesus folded a napkin.

Consider also the incident described in John 20:11–18. When Mary Magdalene remained at the tomb, somebody spoke to her. Turning, she thought that she was asking the gardener where the body of Jesus had been taken. The figure standing before her said, "Mary." She recognized Him immediately by the way that He pronounced her name—those little human recognitions.

Look also at the account of the two disciples on the road to Emmaus as recorded in Luke 24:30–31. A stranger sat down to break bread with them at supper time. They asked the stranger who seemed so knowledgeable about the Scriptures if He would say the prayer of blessing. As He said the blessing, they recognized Him. They recognized the way Jesus said a blessing at the table.

In the story of the disciples who were out on the Sea of

Galilee, when the person standing in the gray mist of the morning on the seashore told them to take the net and transfer it from one side of the little boat to the other side, they did as he said and caught a great school of fish. Then it was that John said to Simon Peter: "Simon, do you know who that is? That is Jesus." A fisher of men—his human recognition.

Of course, when the disciples saw Him, they recognized Him by the print of the nails in His hands and by the scar in His side. Those little things that set Jesus apart are just as true of Him raised from the dead as they were in the days of His flesh.

THEY ALL BELIEVED EXCEPT THOMAS

All of the disciples believed, having been convinced, but there was one skeptic. His name was Thomas, "the twin." I can understand him. I am like him in my own life, and I cannot deny it. Thomas did not believe that a man could rise from the dead. "I do not believe that He is alive because dead men do not rise from the grave," said Thomas. I can understand that. I have never seen a dead man live again.

When the keystone is taken away from the arch, the masonry topples to the ground. When the hub is taken out of the wheel, the wheel collapses. When the breath is taken from the body, the human tabernacle of clay turns back to corruption and to dust. When the silver cord is loosed and the golden bowl is broken and the pitcher is broken at the fountain or the wheel at the cistern, then the body returns to the dust as it was. That describes Thomas. That is the way I am most of the time. Dead men do not arise.

In the account in John 20, when the apostles came to Thomas and said: "Thomas, you do not realize the truth. We have seen Jesus. He is alive. He has risen from the dead!" Thomas said, "No. I do not believe it." Just look at the darkness of his despair. When they pressed upon their fellow apostle, "But He is alive! We have seen Him. Our hands have handled Him," Thomas replied, "I will not believe until I can put my finger into the print of the nails in His hands and thrust my hand into His side."

The next Sunday night when the apostles were gathered in the Upper Room, Jesus suddenly stood in their midst. He turned to Thomas. The amazed gaze and wonderment on the face of Thomas turned to shame as he cast down his eyes. How strange it must have been for Thomas to hear the harsh, crude, physical test that he himself had suggested. He wanted to put his finger into the print of the nails and his hand into Christ's side before he would believe. The Lord said to the shame-faced, sullen unbeliever who had voiced this materialistic ultimatum: "Thomas, put your finger into the print of the nails. Put your hand into the rupture of My side. Be not faithless, but believing." Thomas cried in a great affirmation of faith that comes ultimately out of the hearts of all of us skeptics, "My Lord and my God!" Then Jesus pronounced the benedictory beatitude that is for us all, "Thomas, because thou hast seen me, thou hast believed: blessed [*makarioi,* meaning "happy"] are they that have not seen, and yet have believed" (John 20:29). It is our beatitude. Jesus is alive. We believe it.

His Presence With Them

In those days after His resurrection, Jesus suddenly would appear anywhere at anytime. Suddenly He was standing in the Garden. He was in step on a lonely road. He was present at the supper table. In the Upper Room, with the doors closed, He appeared. On the seashore, on the mountain top, there He was. Suddenly, anywhere, anytime, without announcement, He could be seen. After forty days they did not need to see Him any longer with their eyes. They knew by His presence with them that Jesus was alive. He closed His Great Commission with the incomparable promise, "And, lo, I am with you alway, even unto the end of the age]." He is with us; He is alive.

The first martyr, Stephen, when he was stoned to death, lifted up his face to heaven and he saw Jesus at the right hand of the Father. He is alive!

Saul of Tarsus was breathing out threatening and slaughter against the disciples of Christ, yet on the road to Damascus above the brilliant shining of the noonday sun Jesus stood in the way.

With the sainted apostle John, left on the Isle of Patmos to die of exposure and starvation in exile, He was there. Jesus is alive!

His Presence Is With Us Through the Years

Through these years, with the generations since, Jesus has been in our midst. He lives. Jesus is with us in obedient service.

However feeble our dedicated efforts may be, Jesus is with us serving and working. He is alive. He is here.

In the heart of central Africa, I stood looking at the tremendous gargantuan statue of the missionary David Livingstone. The statue faces the Zambezi River where the river falls over a gigantic precipice down four hundred feet to the chasm below—a mile-wide river, the Victoria Falls. As I stood there looking at that gigantic statue of David Livingstone, facing the Zambezi River and the Victoria Falls, I can imagine how it was when he first looked upon them. Going down the Zambezi, seeking an ultimate entrance into Central Africa from the Eastern Coast, the friendly tribe with whom he was then journeying said to him, "Down that river are ferocious and vicious enemies, and they will not let you pass. At the peril of your life you go further."

David Livingstone had a little idiosyncrasy. When time came to make a decision, he would pray. Then he would take his Bible, open it, look at the verse to which it opened, and that would be God's answer to his prayer. Not knowing whether to proceed down the river or to refrain, he took it to God. In prayer he laid it before the Lord. He took his Bible, opened it, and then looked at the verse to which it fell open. It was this,

> Teaching them to observe all things whatsoever I have commanded you: and, lo, I am with you alway, even unto the end of the world (Matt. 28:20).

Livingstone turned toward his black retinue and said, "Let's go." With assurance, he went down the Zambezi, finally looking at those glorious falls that he had discovered. Jesus is alive! He will go with you. In obedient service, He pilgrimages by your side.

Jesus is alive! He is with us in that agonizing hour of infinite trial and sorrow. The great far-famed pastor who stood behind the pulpit of First Baptist Church, Dallas, for forty-seven years had a wonderful friend in the congregation. Captain J. C. Arnold was first the Captain of the Texas Rangers and later the Chief of Police for the city of Dallas. Dr. Truett and Captain Arnold were in Johnson County on a bird hunt. The captain walked in front of Dr. Truett. Then, unthinkingly and inadvertently, Dr. Truett switched his hammerless shotgun from one arm to the other. When he did so, he accidentally touched the trigger and shot the man in front of him—his best friend, Captain Arnold, who died from that wound. The pastor fell into indescribable sorrow. He said that he could never lift his face to preach again. The days passed, and he did not sleep. He was in an agony of soul. One Saturday night, as he slept for the first time in days and nights, Jesus appeared before him. He said to Dr. Truett, "Be not afraid. From this moment you are My preacher."

Dr. Truett awakened and then went back to sleep. The Lord appeared to him again, saying the same words. He went to sleep the third time. The Lord appeared to him, uttering the same words of assurance. Soon the word was sent over the city of Dallas that Truett was preaching again. The other congregations dismissed their services so that all the city might come and listen to the great man of God standing behind that holy pulpit. Jesus is alive! Jesus lives!

He appears to us in invitation and acceptance when we open the doors of our hearts to Him.

> Behold, I stand at the door, and knock: if any man hear my voice, and open the door, I will come in to him, and will sup with him, and he with me (Rev. 3:20).

Can I believe that? How thrilled and excited I would be if at the door of my house would stand a great king or a prime minister or an angel like the one who appeared to Abraham or Zacharias. But the exalted Christ Himself stands at that door knocking. If I open the door, He will come in. But you say, "Pastor, He may knock at the door of your house, of your heart, but He does not knock at my door." Oh, but He does. In every providence of life, Jesus is there seeking entrance into your home, into your heart, into your life. He speaks to us on the pages of the Holy Bible. His face is on every leaf. He appeals to us in every word. These words are the revelation of the presence of Jesus in our midst.

Erasmus, the tremendously gifted German scholar, wrote in the preface to his *Textus Receptus,* the first Greek Testament ever published and the one that is the basis for the translation of the King James Version, these words: "On these pages you will see the face of Jesus. You will see the Lord Himself, the whole Christ, more fully and more completely than if He stood in the flesh before you." We see Jesus in the Holy Scriptures.

Jesus is alive! He is in the midst of a congregation of believers. He said that wherever two or three are gathered together in

His name, there He would be in the midst. Jesus is with us. He is alive!

Jesus is with us in our praise, our praying, and our intercessions. When somebody is converted, when somebody is saved, there is joy in the presence of the angels of God, and I know Jesus is one of them. He is in heaven, and He looks upon us and worships with us on earth. Jesus is alive!

He is with us in all of our trials and disappointments. The Book of Job ends with these words of the great patriarch, "I have heard of thee by the hearing of the ear: but now mine eye seeth thee." Trial and frustration and disappointment and sorrow bring to us a feeling and sensitivity to the nearness of Christ. He is alive.

He is with us in our loneliness. You are never by yourself. I suppose John thought that he was alone when he was exiled to Patmos, there to die. Turning to hear the great voice that spoke behind him, he looked upon the Lord Jesus. In our loneliness, He is always present. He is with us. He is alive.

In all of the providences of life, Jesus is with us. In the day when you built your home, Jesus was present. On the day when your baby was born, Jesus was there. He fashioned the little life and breathed into the child the breath of a living soul. Jesus was there. In that last parting moment at the grave, Jesus is there. We do not leave our beloved dead in the hands of the grave or in the hands of hades or darkness or destruction. We leave our beloved dead in the hands of the blessed Lord Jesus.

When was the first time I was ever introduced to death? For more than fifty years I have been a pastor. Many times I have bowed my head with a sorrowing family. Many times I have committed to the earth a dead body. I began to think back to the first time I ever heard of death and finally to the years of my early childhood in Eldorado, Oklahoma. We left Eldorado when I was five years of age. My father went away on a mission. When he came back, I asked him where he had been. He pulled me to himself and said, "Son, I have been away burying my mother." From him and from others, I found that my grandmother had been a very godly and saintly woman. He told me about the translation of his mother and the memorial service. Then he said, "The song they sang I will sing to you now." My father loved to sing. He used to take those hymns with their old shaped notes and sing hour after hour. So he sang that song to me.

The Great Fact of the Gospel: Jesus Is Alive

Safe in the arms of Jesus,
Safe on His gentle breast.
There by His love o'ershaded,
Sweetly my soul shall rest.

What a comfort and indescribable strength to know that we do not leave beloved dead in the hands of the grave or of death or of darkness or of despair, but we leave them in the arms of Jesus! What a comfort to know that when the day comes for my own translation, it will not be corruption, darkness, and despair that I face. No, I look forward to seeing Jesus face to face! The heart, strength, and glory of the gospel is that in life as in death, in sickness as in health, in poverty as in affluence, in youth as in old age, Jesus is alive! He walks with us, blesses us, works with us. Jesus is alive!

19

Our Own Coming Resurrection

In Acts 26, the apostle Paul presents the defense of his life before Herod Agrippa II:

> Then Agrippa said unto Paul, Thou art permitted to speak for thyself. Then Paul stretched forth the hand, and answered for himself:
> I think myself happy, king Agrippa, because I shall answer for myself this day before thee touching all the things whereof I am accused of the Jews (Acts 26:1–2).

Then as he speaks of the Christian way, he asks:

> Why should it be thought a thing incredible with you, that God should raise the dead? (Acts 26:8)

Is there a resurrection of the dead? Is there life beyond the grave? Robert Ingersoll, a brilliant lecturer of the last century, standing over the body of his dead brother said:

> Life is a narrow vale between the cold and barren peaks of two eternities; we strive in vain to look beyond the heights. We cry aloud, and the only answer is the echo of our wailing cry.

The old patriarch, Job, asks an eternal question, "If a man die, shall he live again?" (Job 14:14a).

There is not one of us who has not asked that question in fear, in hope, in dread, and in agony. I suppose that the question was asked over the first grave and that it has been repeated through all of the centuries since.

The question is emphasized by the great monuments of the

world, each one an attempt to reach toward immortality—life beyond this life. The ancient pyramids of Egypt are tombs. The mausoleum at Halicarnassus was one of the ancient wonders of the world, and it was, like the pyramids, a tomb. The Taj Mahal in Agra, India, the most beautifully effective building I have ever seen in the world, is a tomb. The tombs of the emperors of ancient Japan in Nara and Kyoto stand as monuments to the hope of an immortal life. The tomb of Napoleon in Paris, France, the tomb of St. Peter's Cathedral, the Vatican in Rome, the great basilicas of St. Paul's and Westminster Abbey in which are entombed the great of the British empire—all of these emphasize the hope and desire of the human soul for immortality.

If a man die, shall he live again? The waste of death is devastating and universal. Neither the Goth, the Vandal, the Hun, the Tartar, nor the Saracen ever slew so mercilessly. There is no pity for the young, no mercy for the old, and no regard for the good, the true, and the beautiful in the devastation of death.

Death's presence brings such finality. All of us feel it. Standing before a newly dug grave or being introduced for the first time to the dissolution of your family circle—these that we have loved and known in our family group—all of it presses upon our hearts with such devastation. The very appearance and approach of the pale horseman strikes terror to our souls. We peer into the darkness of the grave and repeat Job's ancient question: "If I die, do I live again?"

The Immortality of the Soul

As we read and study and search in our own hearts, there are two answers to that question. One can be found in human history in the undying hope of the nature of man, and that answer concerns the immortality of the soul. It is an unfading and undying hope in the human spirit. All of the passing ages neither blunt it nor dissuade us from it.

Cicero has brought down to us from ancient history the most exhaustive study of that subject. He concluded with this sentence: "The immortality of the soul is the belief of all peoples." That conclusion of the ancient Roman senator and orator is confirmed by everything that we know. When finally we were able to decipher the ancient hieroglyphics, the picture writing of Egypt, it was discovered that those writings concerned the dead and were called, "The Book of the Dead." The book described the life beyond the grave. When finally we were able to decipher that ancient cuneiform, the wedge-shaped writing of the ancient Akkadian, Sumerian, and Babylonian peoples, we saw that it also concerned the life beyond the grave.

Immortality is the subject of Homer in his *Iliad* and *Odyssey*. It is the inspiration of Virgil in his *Aeneid*. The ancient Greek warrior was buried with his armor because he would need it in his other life. The painted American Indian was buried with his bow and his arrow so that it could be part of his life in the "happy hunting grounds." There are no tribes so degraded in central Africa, or among the Patagonians at the tip of South America, but that they hold this hope in their hearts. The passing of the ages and the centuries has not deterred the human spirit from the belief that there is a life beyond the grave.

All of the thinking and writing of the great rationalistic philosophers of mankind have not dissuaded us from a belief in the immortality of the soul. Against such a belief Jean Paul Richter, the eighteenth-century German author and philosopher wrote:

> I have traversed the world, I have risen to the sun, I have pressed athwart the great waste places of the sky. I have descended to the place where the very shadow cast by being dies out and ends. We are orphans, you and I. Every soul in this vast corpse-trench of the universe is utterly alone.

The eloquent British philosopher, mathematician, and author, Bertrand Russell added these words of skepticism:

> That man is the product of causes which had no pre-vision of the end they were achieving; that his origin, his growth, his hopes, his fears, his loves, and beliefs, are but the outcome of the accidental collocation of atoms; that no fire, no heroism, no intensity of thought and feeling can preserve an individual life beyond the grave; that all the labors of the ages, all the noonday brightness of human genius are destined to extinction in the vast death of the solar system, and that the whole temple of man's achievement must inevitably be buried beneath the debris of a universe in ruins—all these things, if not beyond dispute, are yet so nearly certain, that no philosophy which rejects them can hope to stand. Only within the scaffolding of despair can the soul's habitation henceforth be built.

This is the conclusion of the rationalists through all of the years. Today we call it secular humanism. There is no God. There is no resurrection. There is no immortality. There is no life beyond the grave. And yet, after the centuries of this teaching and after the utmost diatribes of the rationalists, the hope and belief in immortality is as vibrant in the human heart today as it ever was. It is undying.

Somehow, someway, life persuades itself that it is like a great arch, and the life of this world is on the great supporting pillar on this side, and the other pillar upon which the arch stands is in the world to come. Life persuades itself that it is like a gigantic bridge, and on this side is the great pier upon which it is anchored here. The bridge does not stop in the middle above the abyss, but it goes over and beyond and is anchored on a great pier on the other side of the grave. That is the human heart and the human spirit. It never changes.

As we look ahead and peer beyond the darkness of the grave, somehow intimations of immortality may be sufficient for fanciful poetry, but when the room is darkened and the baffled physician is forced to admit defeat, surely we need some certain word that can comfort and strengthen our hearts.

One of the most pathetic utterances of ancient literature is the cry of Plato in the presence of death:

> Oh, that there were some divine word upon which we could more securely and less perilously sail upon a stronger vessel.

As Plato looked out into the darkness beyond the River Styx, he sought some revelation from heaven that would be a strong raft, a vessel upon which his soul might launch out across the sea of eternity and into the world that is to come.

"If a man die, shall he live again?" The answer of human history and of the undying hope of the soul is, "There is an immortality, there is a life beyond the grave."

THE CHRISTIAN REVELATION OF THE RESURRECTION OF THE DEAD

It was Christ who brought life and immortality to light. Before Him, it was a vague hope, a shadowy belief, an insubstantial substance, a peripheral reaching, a peering into the darkness, a prayer, a cry. But in Christ the persuasion took firm and undying substance. It became a revelation from heaven.

There are many great biblical scholars who avow that the high-water mark of all revelation is 1 Corinthians 15—the great revelation of God concerning the resurrection of the dead.

175

Now if Christ be preached that he rose from the dead, how say some among you that there is no resurrection of the dead?

But if there be no resurrection of the dead, then is Christ not risen:

And if Christ be not risen, then is our preaching vain, and your faith is also vain.

Yea, and we are found false witnesses of God; because we have testified of God that he raised up Christ: whom he raised not up, if so be that the dead rise not.

For if the dead rise not, then is not Christ raised:

And if Christ be not raised, your faith is vain; ye are yet in your sins.

Then they also which are fallen asleep in Christ are perished. [These who before us have died, have died in hopelessness, in interminable and unmitigated darkness.]

If in this life only we have hope in Christ, we are of all men most miserable.

But now is Christ risen from the dead, and become the first fruits of them that slept.

For since by man came death, by man came also the resurrection of the dead.

For as in Adam all die [Born in sin, conceived in iniquity, the backdrop of condemnation and judgment in all the bloodstreams of the human family], even so in Christ shall all be made alive (1 Cor. 15:12–22).

That is the heart and the substance of the Christian faith.

Job now can arise from his ash heap and say with a tremendously triumphant voice:

For I know that my redeemer liveth, and that he shall stand at the latter day upon the earth:

And though after my skin worms destroy this body, yet in my flesh shall I see God:

Whom I shall see for myself, and mine eyes shall behold, and not another (Job 19:25–27a).

The psalmist now can take his harp from the willow tree. The king can exchange his sackcloth for garments of beauty and glory. Nehemiah can cease his weeping. Daniel can arise from his knees. Jesus is alive! He has risen from the dead! He is the firstfruits of them that sleep. In our time and in our day, we also will be raised in the likeness of His glorious Resurrection. That is the Christian faith.

Another meaningful passage that Paul writes and a question that he answers is found in 1 Corinthians 15,

> But some man will say, How are the dead raised up? and with
> what body do they come? (v. 35).

That is a very legitimate question. What kind of people will
we be? What kind of bodies will we have? Will "you" be "you"
and will "I" be "I," or will we be some kind of a metamorphic
creature far removed from us? Does the Resurrection mean that I
will live and it will be I and that you will live and it will be you?

The immortality of the soul, as I have tried to avow, is a
universal persuasion of the whole human race through all of its
history. By the feeble light of nature, even the most degraded
tribes of the earth were able to see that there is a life beyond the
grave. But the doctrine of the resurrection of the body, that we
shall live personally, identifiably, and individually is peculiar to
Christianity. No other faith ever dared to avow it. This doctrine of
the resurrection of the body is presented by the Christian believer
alone.

When Paul stood on Mars Hill, speaking to the Areopagus,
the highest court of the Athenians, had he discussed the immortality of the soul, all of the Stoic and Epicurean philosophers
would have been eager to listen to him and to discuss it. That is
what they argued about in their ultimate speculations. What of
the soul? Is it immortal? They would have listened with eager
attention to a discussion of the immortality of the soul. But when
Paul spoke of the resurrection of the dead, the Epicureans
laughed and burst into scoffing. It was ridiculous to them. The
Stoics, being more generous and courteous, bowed themselves
out saying, "We will hear from you of this matter later," and they
left.

The doctrine of the resurrection of the dead is the heart of
the Christian message, and it finds its basis in the resurrection of
Jesus Christ. He arose from among the dead, the actual man,
Christ Jesus. It is *He* with the nail prints in His hands and feet,
with the scar in His side, who lived again. It is He whom they
crucified who is now risen from the grave. That is the Christian
faith.

The Christian message of hope and salvation is that we who
trust in Christ shall be raised together with Him. It will be you; it
will be I. Paul will not be Isaiah, and Isaiah will not be Jeremiah.
In the Resurrection it will be Isaiah, Jeremiah, and Paul. John
Chrysostom will not be George Whitefield, and George White-

177

field will not be Charles Haddon Spurgeon. It will be Chrysostom, the golden-mouthed preacher. It will be George Whitefield, God's great evangelist. It will be Charles Spurgeon, God's great pastor. Identity is not lost.

Identification is the key of this passage that Paul writes in answering that question, "In what body shall we live?"

> But God giveth it a body as it hath pleased him, and to every seed his own body.
>
> All flesh is not the same flesh: but there is one kind of flesh of men, another flesh of beasts, another of fishes, and another of birds.
>
> There are also celestial bodies, and bodies terrestrial: but the glory of the celestial is one, and the glory of the terrestrial is another.
>
> There is one glory of the sun, and another glory of the moon, and another glory of the stars: for one star differeth from another star in glory.
>
> So also is the resurrection of the dead. [You will be you, and I will be I, and we are different from each other. Each one of us will be identifiable in the Resurrection.] It is sown in corruption; it is raised in incorruption:
>
> It is sown in dishonor; it is raised in glory: it is sown in weakness; it is raised in power:
>
> It is sown a natural body; it is raised a spiritual body (1 Cor. 15:38–44a).

We have a material body for this life and this world, but God is fashioning for us a spiritual body for the world that is to come. That is an amazing contradiction in words: a spiritual body. Those two words are antithetical. They are mutually contradictory—spirit and body. But in the Resurrection, God is framing for us a spiritual body. It is something that God does.

In my human mind I do not understand that. A man is buried in the ground, and a great oak thrusts its roots through his physical frame, and the substance of the man is turned into leaves or fruit. Or the man is eaten up by a fish, and the man turns into the scales and teeth of a fish. How is it that God raises this body from the dead? It is something that God does. God marks the molecules and the atoms of this physical substance, the human frame in which my soul lives, and in the resurrection from the dead God gathers it together, and I live in His sight.

In the early Christian centuries, there was a mythological faith religion that spread over the Graeco-Roman world. Coming out of Egypt, it was the worship of Isis and Osiris. Osiris' body was dismembered, fragmentized, and scattered over the whole earth, but Isis lovingly, tenderly, fondly gathered all the pieces together, and the god was resurrected and reborn and lived again. That is mythological. That is an ancient and dead religion.

But they had a shadow of a truth in the affirmation that those who believed in Isis and Osiris would be immortal. The full revelation is in Jesus Christ. God is able to gather up the fragments of our lives, the substance of this physical frame, and He is able to recreate it, to regenerate it. We are born again and we live in His sight. The resurrection of the dead—it is God who does it.

That is why the apostle writes in the marvelous concluding consummation of 1 Corinthians 15,

> Thanks be to God, which giveth us the victory through our Lord Jesus Christ (v. 57).

Can the dead raise themselves? No! They are dead. But the Holy Spirit can do for us what we are unable to do for ourselves. The Holy Spirit of God raised Jesus from the dead (Rom. 1:4). The same Holy Spirit of God will raise us from the dead. The Holy Spirit lives in our bodies as His temple, and we do not bury the Holy Spirit. By the Holy Spirit we are all baptized into the body of Christ. We are made one with the Lord by the Holy Spirit. We belong to His body, and His body does not see corruption. When we accept our Lord, the Holy Spirit comes and lives in our physical frame. This is the temple of the Holy Spirit of God, and the Holy Spirit who raised up Christ is the same power who will raise us up. We are members of the body of Christ and are imperishable. We will live forever in Him. It is something God does.

Do you notice one other thing? Not only does Paul say the Holy Spirit of God will raise us up from the dead, but the apostle makes another marvelous avowal:

> Behold, I show you a mystery; We shall not all sleep, but we shall all be changed,
> In a moment, in the twinkling of an eye, at the last trump: for the trumpet shall sound, and the dead shall be raised incorruptible, and we shall be changed (1 Cor. 15:51–52).

Think of it! We shall all be changed.

In the days of the bloody Queen Mary, two martyrs were tied to the stake. One was lame and the other was blind. As the fires were lit, the lame man threw away his crutch and turned to

179

his companion and said, "Courage, brother, this fire will heal us both!"

We will all be changed. The blind will see, the lame will walk, the old will be young, and the feeble will be made strong. We all will be recreated in the glorious likeness of our Savior. This is the Christian faith. There is life aboundingly glorious in Christ, even beyond the grave! "He that liveth and believeth in me shall never, ever die."

> O precious cross!
> O glorious crown!
> O resurrection day!
> Ye angels, from the stars come down
> And bear my soul away.

20

Our Lord's Entrance Into Heaven

> Wherefore he saith, When he ascended up on high, he led captivity captive, and gave gifts unto men.
>
> (Now that he ascended, what is it but that he also descended first into the lower parts of the earth?
>
> He that descended is the same also that ascended up far above all heavens, that he might fill all things) (Eph. 4:8–10).

There are eight great epochs in the life of our Savior:

    (1) His eternal preexistence in heaven
    (2) His descent to the earth, i.e., His virgin birth
    (3) His mighty ministry
    (4) His atoning death on the cross
    (5) His resurrection
    (6) His ascension into heaven
    (7) His triumphant and kingly return
    (8) His eternal reign in heaven and in earth.

Of those eight, His descent into the earth and His ascent into heaven—that heaven of heavens, the third heaven—is like Jacob's ladder. The Bible names the heavens: the first heaven where the birds fly and the clouds go by; the second heaven of the sidereal spheres, the milky ways, and the stars that shine; then the heaven of heavens where God's throne is forever set, to which heaven our Lord has ascended.

We will look at the Ascension in four ways: (1) as we view it from the earth, (2) as the angels watched it in heaven, (3) as the

Old Testament saints waited in promise, and (4) as the New Testament church, the bride of Christ, receives her bridegroom.

As We View Our Lord's Ascension From Earth

In 1 Peter 1:20 and in Revelation 13:8, our Lord is described as the Lamb slain from before the foundation of the earth. In Hebrews 10, we have presented a scene in the primordial existence of time when the Christ, the Captain of the hosts of heaven, volunteered to redeem a coming, fallen humanity. In the foreknowledge of God, He saw the rebellion of Lucifer, the fall of our first parents, and the despair and waste of the world. As a result of the rebellion and sin of Satan in heaven, God's beautiful creation became a world of waste and void. The earth became an immeasurable cemetery in which we bury our dead. It groans and travails in agony until now.

In the midst of that fall, there was given to the fallen human race a *protevangelium,* "a gospel before the gospel."

> And I will put enmity between thee and the woman, and between thy seed and her seed; it shall bruise thy head, and thou shalt bruise his heel (Gen. 3:15).

The seed of the woman would destroy, bruise, and crush Satan's head. The rest of the Bible is the carrying out in God's faithfulness that promise of a deliverer and a redeemer.

The Savior was to come through the line of Seth, not Cain. He was to come through the line of Noah and Shem. He was to come through the line of Abraham, Isaac, and Jacob, and through the line of Judah. He was to be a member of the house and family of David, and the prophecies thereafter describe the beauty, the preciousness, the comfort, the deliverance, and the glory of His reign.

In keeping with that holy promise of God, in the fullness of time, He was born of a woman. Then followed His ministry of deed and word, His atoning death, His resurrection from among the dead, and His ascension into heaven.

> And when he had spoken these things, while they beheld, he was taken up: and a cloud [the *shekinah* glory of God] received him out of their sight (Acts 1:9).

That is the way the story reads as we view the ascension of our Lord from the earth.

Our Lord's Entrance Into Heaven

AS THE ANGELS WATCHED FROM HEAVEN

In the rebellion of Lucifer in the dim ages of the ages past, one third of the angelic hosts of heaven chose to follow Satan (Rev. 12:4), but two-thirds of them were true, loyal, and faithful to their Crown Prince, the preexistent Lord Jesus Christ, the second person of the Trinity, the eternal God. In that rebellion, two-thirds of those angels in heaven were made aware of God's redemptive plan, but they could not understand it.

First Peter 1:12 says that the angels desired to look into what God was doing. It was an astonishing and indescribably amazing providence when they saw their Crown Prince of glory, the preexistent Christ, God Himself, come down into the womb of a virgin girl named Mary to be born as one of us—a man. All through the life of our Lord the angels watched in amazement. Paul says,

> Great is the mystery [*musterion*] of godliness: God was manifest in the flesh, justified in the Spirit, seen of angels, preached unto the Gentiles, believed on in the world, received up into glory (1 Tim. 3:16).

The angels watched over our Lord all through the days of His ministry. When He was born, they sang in countless numbers a song of praise and glory. It meant the deliverance of the fallen race and the restoration of this destroyed and wasted world. They sang at the coming of our Lord into the earth. They were present helping our Savior in His temptation. They comforted Him in Gethsemane. When He was raised from the dead, they were at the foot and at the head of the grave. When He ascended into glory, they announced to the waiting, gazing, looking-upward apostles that this same Jesus whom they were receiving into glory was some day coming again. They watched our Lord and received Him into heaven. Can you imagine the scene in glory when their Prince, the Captain of the hosts of heaven, returned in triumph! It is beyond our imagination. What a scene it must have been!

In Psalm 24, we have a record of that scene in prophecy:

> Lift up your heads, O ye gates; and be ye lifted up, ye everlasting doors; and the King of glory shall come in.
> Who is this King of glory? The LORD strong and mighty, the LORD mighty in battle (vv. 7–8).

183

Concerning those principalities and powers under Satan who warred against our Christ, the Scripture says,

> And having spoiled principalities and powers, he made a show of them openly, triumphing over them in it (Col. 2:15).

Our text says, "He ascended up on high, leading captivity captive" (Eph. 4:8). To His chariot wheels is tied our conquered enemy, Satan. He is now a toothless and stingless dragon. He is a defeated, crushed, and conquered foe.

When our Lord entered heaven, He entered as the great conqueror of him who had brought rebellion among the angels, the one who had introduced sin into God's holy creation and destroyed the universe and our world, and finally the one who had encompassed the death of our first parents and the human race. When the Lord entered into heaven amidst the song, praise, and exaltation of ten thousand times ten thousands of angels, what a scene it must have been!

Look at this passage, "He ascended on high leading captivity captive." Those who had held Him captive, He now has in His possession as captives—Satan in league with sin and death. He became sin for us that we might be the righteousness of God in Him. He entered into the grave that He might win there for us an eternal and everlasting victory. The bands of sin and the bonds of death He broke asunder, and He arose from the dead and entered into heaven, the great creator, victor, and conqueror of the enemies we have known in our lives—sin, death, the grave, and all of the hurts and sorrows of existence. Can you imagine what a scene it must have been when the angels received back into glory their Crown Prince, the preexistent Christ, the Lord and Captain of their hosts, and our own loving Savior!

As the Old Testament Saints Waited in Promise

In the midst of the story of the transfiguration of our Lord, we read:

> And as he prayed, the fashion of his countenance was altered, and his raiment was white and glistering [the deity of our Lord covered over by His flesh is shining through].
> And, behold, there talked with him two men, which were Moses and Elijah:
> Who appeared in glory, and spake of his decease which he should accomplish at Jerusalem (Luke 9:29–31).

Far more is in that text than we would discern by reading it in an English translation. Moses and Elijah were appearing to Christ in glory, speaking to Jesus of His "decease" (*exodus*) which He would accomplish and bring to fulfillment (*plēroō*) according to prophecy.

What does that mean? Moses represents those who would die and be buried. Elijah represents those who would be raptured and translated, those who would be changed in a moment, in the twinkling of an eye.

Both Moses and Elijah spoke to our Lord about the *exodos.* That is what God calls the deliverance of His people out of the bondage of Egypt. The second book in the Bible God called Exodus, and it speaks of the great *exodos,* the deliverance of the people from the bondage of death and corruption into the glorious liberty of the sons of God, which He would bring to pass and accomplish (*plēroō*) in Jerusalem in fulfillment of all of the prophecies of the Old Testament.

When the Old Testament saints died, the Bible says they were gathered to their fathers. Abraham was gathered to his fathers. Isaac and Jacob, David and Solomon—all the Old Testament saints were gathered to their fathers, awaiting the redemption, the atoning death of our Savior.

When Moses and Elijah spoke to our Lord, they said: "Jesus, we are in heaven, awaiting the fulfillment of the promise. It is because of Your atoning death that we have hope of deliverance, of the forgiveness of sins, and of a home in glory. Our eternal life and destiny are in Your hands through this holy, atoning purpose that You will realize for us in Jerusalem on the cross."

Can you imagine, therefore, the infinite ecstasy, delight, and exaltation of the Old Testament saints with Moses and Elijah when they received our Lord upon His ascension! He had died for their sins; He had delivered them from the judgment of death, and He had made it possible for them to enter into heaven. He was conqueror over sin, death, and the grave! He was victor and deliverer!

The Old Testament saints arose in exultation to greet Him when He returned to heaven! There is Abel with his righteous offering. There is Noah with his sermon on repentance. There is Abraham with his heart in the Promised Land. There is David with his harp. There is Elijah with his fire. There is Isaiah with his prophecies of comfort. There is Ezekiel with his four cherubim.

There is Daniel untouched by his hungry lions. There is Zechariah with his quietness and his confidence. There is Malachi bowing before the Son of Righteousness who comes with healing in His wings. What a glorious day it must have been when the Old Testament saints arose to receive their great deliverer and Savior, the Lord Jesus, the Christ!

AS THE NEW TESTAMENT CHURCH RECEIVED THEIR LORD

When you read the first chapters of the Apocalypse, the language groans under the heavy assignment of describing our Lord's reception into glory. When the redeemed, when the four cherubim, when the twenty-four elders (twelve of the Old Testament and twelve of the New Testament, the patriarchs and the apostles) received their Lord and joined in the song of Moses and the Lamb, it is beyond description. Oh, what a day it must have been when Jesus returned to glory! Unto Him who loved us and washed us from our sins in His own blood, unto Him be glory and honor forever and forever! Hallelujah! Amen!

The apostle Paul wrote of the eternal exaltation of our Lord:

> Wherefore God also hath highly exalted him, and given him a name which is above every name [above every archangel, above every angel, above all of God's creation]:
> That at the name of Jesus every knee should bow, of things in heaven, and things in earth, and things under the earth;
> And that every tongue should confess that Jesus Christ is Lord, to the glory of God the Father (Phil. 2:9–11).

Everything in heaven above belongs to Him. Everything around Him is His—the earth and its glory—all belong to Him. Everything in His church—His redeemed family, all of us—belong to Him. In that nether world of the infernal, the damned, and the demons, they also will acknowledge Him. Every knee will bow and every tongue will confess that Jesus Christ is Lord, to the glory of God the Father. Oh, what a day it must have been when all the saints of heaven, God's redeemed church, welcomed their Savior and their Lord!

One time I read of a city in America with a large municipal auditorium. Somebody had the unusual idea of asking the finest representatives of the living religions of the world, two of them each night, to present their faith. It thrilled and delighted the interested people of the city, and they jammed that great auditorium by the thousands. One night representatives of the Shinto and Hindu religions presented their faiths. Another night representatives of Islam or Muhammadanism and Judaism presented their respective faiths. The last night Buddhism and Christianity were presented.

The representative of the Buddhist faith was a brilliant and gifted man, and he swayed that vast audience with his words of oratory and peroration, speaking of Nirvana and of all the disciplines and meditation from the life of Buddha.

He was followed by the representative of the Christian faith, but somehow the man stumbled and stammered and our Lord was presented poorly, weakly, and ineffectively. As the man stammeringly spoke, suddenly in the upper balcony a man began to sing:

> All hail the power of Jesus' name!
> Let angels prostrate fall;
> Bring forth the royal diadem,
> And crown Him Lord of all.

Another man on the other side took it up, and still others joined in:

> Ye chosen seed of Israel's race,
> Ye ransomed from the fall,
> Hail Him who saves you by His grace,
> And crown Him Lord of all.

Then the whole throng of thousands began to sing:

> Let every kindred, every tribe,
> On this terrestrial ball,
> To Him all majesty ascribe,
> And crown Him Lord of all.

Jesus is Lord. Jesus is King. Jesus is Conqueror. He is God preexistent. He is God manifest in the flesh. He is God, triumphant and conquering over sin, the grave, and death. He is our Lord reigning at the right hand of majesty on high. He is our great God and Savior who will appear some day apart from sin. He is our manifest and eternal Lord, the recreator and restorer of this wasted world. What a marvel God has given to us who are made out of dust—the privilege of being a fellow heir with Him, a brother in the household of faith, a member of the family of God! Jesus is Lord!

187

21

The Entrance of Our Lord Beyond the Veil

> That by two immutable things, in which it was impossible for God to lie, we might have a strong consolation, who have fled for refuge to lay hold upon the hope set before us:
> Which hope we have as an anchor of the soul, both sure and steadfast, and which entereth into that within the veil;
> Whither the forerunner is for us entered, even Jesus, made an high priest (Heb. 6:18–20).

THE EARTHLY SANCTUARY IS A TYPE

In Hebrews 9, the author picks up the theme he has introduced in chapter 6. He writes at great length upon the entrance of our Lord beyond the veil.

The first ten verses describe what the author calls "the earthly sanctuary." The first covenant had ordinances of divine service and an earthly (*kosmikos*) sanctuary made in pattern after the one in heaven—our eternal sanctuary. The earthly one is like the one in heaven.

Then the author describes that *kosmikos* sanctuary—the tabernacle. The verses that follow describe its furniture and its vessels and speak of the Day of Atonement when once each year the high priest, with blood of bulls and goats, entered into the Holy of Holies.

Then in verse 11, the author describes Christ who enters into the Holy of Holies once for all to obtain redemption for us beyond the veil.

The rest of the chapter speaks of what Christ has wrought for us in that eternal redemption beyond that beautiful and sacred tapestry. The tabernacle and the Levitical sacrifices of the Old Testament were types and pictures and figures and adumbrations of the atoning work of our Lord.

God is teaching us in pictorial form what He is preparing to do for our salvation, and He is teaching us the nomenclature or vocabulary of heaven. Here on earth we talk in terms of fields and fruits, business and investments, and houses and land. That is our language here. The language of heaven is propitiation, atonement, expiation, altar, sacrifice, and intercession. God taught us the meaning of those words in types and figures just as we teach our children. We have pictures that represent something that we are trying to teach our children. Everything has a name, and we teach the child the words by way of the picture. Thus God did with us in the tabernacle on this earth.

He names the tabernacle accordingly. There is a gate into the court, and on the inside of the gate there is the brazen altar of sacrifice. Beyond the altar, there is the laver, and beyond the laver, there is the door into the sanctuary, the Holy Place. To the south, on the left, there is the seven-branched lampstand of gold; to the north, on the right, is the table of shewbread; directly in front and before the veil is the golden altar of incense. Then there is the tapestry in between, and beyond the veil there is the presence of God—the ark of the covenant, the mercy seat, and the cherubim, whose overarching wings touched as they looked down upon the mercy seat of God.

Without fail and without exception, God is pictured in the Old Testament as being separated and hidden from man. Our sins have made a division between us and God. He is on one side of the tapestry, and we are on the other side. Just once a year a representative man, the high priest, lifted up the veil and entered into that sanctum with the blood of propitiation.

All of the feasts and festivals and holy days of the Jewish nation were glad occasions. They were happy days, joyous days. The Levitical code demanded that just one day out of the year the people were to afflict their souls with the remembrance of the judgment of God upon sin. Today that is called Yom Kippur, the Day of Atonement. On that day, the representative man, the high priest, appeared before the Lord with blood.

ACCESS IS BEYOND THE VEIL

The teaching of the Scripture in that tabernacle is very faithful to the reality of God. He is hidden from us. He is on the other side of the curtain. Our sins have divided us from Him. Isaiah so eloquently described this.

> Behold, the LORD's hand is not shortened, that it cannot save; neither his ear heavy, that it cannot hear:
> But your iniquities have separated between you and your God, and your sins have hid his face from you, that he will not hear (Is. 59:1–2).

God is always presented in the Old Testament as hidden, separate, beyond the veil, and on the other side of the curtain. But at the same time, there is a beautiful and pictorial promise of entrance and access.

Note that the separation is not a brick wall. It is not even made of cedar wood overlaid with pure gold, but it is a veil, a tapestry, a curtain. Woven into that tapestry are figures—cherubim. Without exception, wherever in the Bible cherubim appear, they are figures and symbols of God's grace, mercy, and loving forgiveness. Not only was the division between God and man a tapestry, but it could be lifted. Once year it was raised for the high priest to enter. That is a token and a promise that someday a way of access would be made manifest.

So it is that the author comes to Hebrews 9:11 and speaks of the marvelous, startling, and wonderful fulfillment of all those pictures and types in Jesus our Lord.

> But Christ being come a high priest of good things to come, by a greater and more perfect tabernacle, not made with hands, that is to say, not of this building;
> Neither by the blood of goats and calves, but by his own blood he entered in once into the holy place having obtained eternal redemption for us.
> For if the blood of bulls and of goats, and the ashes of an heifer sprinkling the unclean, sanctifieth to the purifying of the flesh:
> How much more shall the blood of Christ, who through the eternal Spirit offered himself without spot to God, purge your conscience from dead works to serve the living God? (Heb. 9:11–14).

That is an amazing account of the coming of God, incarnate in flesh, into this world. He stands with us on this side of the veil. Though He is Lord and though He is God, He does not stand on the other side of the veil. Rather, He stands on this side of the veil with us who are sinful men and women. He stands in our place.

The altar was in the court, and when the sin offering was made to God, the body was burned outside the gate, outside the camp. Thus, our Lord was sacrificed on this side of the veil where we are, and He suffered outside the gate. Between Him and the Father hung that tapestry, dark and heavy. He cried, "My God, my God, why hast thou forsaken me? *E-li, E-li, la-ma sa-bach-tha-ni?*" And the light of the world went out. The sun refused to shine. Christ was our representative man in sacrifice on this side of the veil.

Then in Hebrews 10 we see the marvel of salvation.

> By a new and living way, which he hath consecrated for us, through the veil, that is to say, his flesh (Heb. 10:20).

When our Lord's body was torn, when our Lord was sacrificed, the veil was rent in two—not from bottom to top as though a man had pulled it apart, but from top to bottom as though God had done it. In the torn flesh and the broken body, in the sacrifice of our Lord, the veil between us and God was rent in two. Had it just been lifted, it could have fallen back again, but being torn and rent, it hung limp on each side. The way into heaven is open and clear, unobstructed to sinful man. Our Lord entered into the sanctuary of heaven, not with the blood of bulls and of goats, but with His own blood to make atonement (at-one-ment) for (between) us and God.

His Entrance Was Once for All

Then the author of Hebrews describes that efficacious salvation that the Lord has won for us in His entrance beyond the veil. He says it is effective, able, and mighty forever. It is a forever thing that our Lord has done. He used two words to describe what our Savior's work is like, having entered beyond the veil. He speaks of His sacrifice as being "once for all." He loves to emphasize that word "once" (*hapax*). He uses it seven times.

> For this he did once [*hapax*] when he offered up himself (Heb. 7:27b).

> Neither by the blood of goats and calves, but by his own blood he entered in once [*hapax*] into the holy place (Heb. 9:12a).

191

But now once [*hapax*] in the end of the world hath he appeared to put away sin by the sacrifice of himself.

And as it is appointed unto men once [*hapax*] to die, but after this the judgment.

So Christ was once [*hapax*] offered to bear the sins of many (Heb. 9:26b–28a).

Because that the worshipers once [*hapax*] purged should have had no more conscience of sins.

By the which will we are sanctified through the offering of the body of Jesus Christ once [*hapax*] for all (Heb. 10:2, 10).

It is a forever atonement that our Lord has made—one time and that one time is sufficient forever.

He uses the illustration that men die one time, not twice. Every man who dies, dies one time. So Christ died one time. The sacrifices that were offered in the tabernacle in type were repeated again and again. But this sacrifice of Christ is sufficient for all time and forever—once, just once.

In the Old Testament, a leprous house was burned down one time. It never needed to be burned down again. So the atoning sacrifice of our Lord was offered to God once, and it never needs to be repeated. In fulfillment of that prophecy, the typology that looked forward to the sacrifice of Christ, all of the sacrifices have been done away.

That to me is one of the most amazing fulfillments of Scripture that you could read anywhere in the history of the world. When the author of Hebrews wrote those words, there were sacrifices and altars on every high hill in the earth. There was the sacrificial altar in Jerusalem on Mt. Moriah in the court of the temple. There were those altars in Ephesus, Antioch, Athens, Rome, Alexandria, and in every town and city in the Graeco-Roman empire. On every high hill you would find an altar and a sacrifice and the smoke reaching up toward the sky. But in this one sacrifice, all of the sacrifices were done away. I have never seen any altar or any sacrifice on any altar in any city in which I have ever been in the world. I have been around the world three times, I have seen thousands of thousands of villages, and I have never seen an altar in any of them. I have looked at thousands and thousands of hills, and I have never seen an altar on the top of one of them. There is one great sacrifice for sin, once for all, and that sacrifice was offered by Jesus our Lord one time. All of the other types and figures were fulfilled in Him, the all-sufficient Sacrifice.

REDEMPTION WAS OBTAINED UNTO ETERNITY

Not only that, but the author avows that in the atoning blood of our Savior, as He entered into that Holy of Holies, He obtained eternal redemption for us. The author loves to use that word "eternal" (*aionios*).

> Neither by the blood of goats and calves, but by his own blood he entered in once into the holy place, having obtained eternal [*aionios*] redemption for us.
>
> How much more shall the blood of Christ, who through the eternal [*aionios*] Spirit offered himself without spot to God, purge your conscience from dead works to serve the living God.
>
> And for this cause he is the mediator of the new testament, that by means of death, for the redemption of the transgressions that were under the first testament, they which are called might receive the promise of eternal [*aionios*] inheritance (Heb. 9:12, 14–15).

Redemption is an eternal thing in the mind of God. It is not an afterthought. In the unnamed, unknown ages past, redemption, salvation, and deliverance were in the heart of God. All creation moves toward redemption. All of the providences that we know in life move toward redemption. All of the voices that God has created have in them an undertone of redemption. It is at the heart of God's purpose for the universe. It is not an expedient by which God proposes to snatch the world from some unprecedented, unforseen accident. It is not the patching up of a broken-down purpose in the mind of God. It is the great purpose of God from the beginning.

An issue of *National Geographic Magazine* had one of those long studies about the universe and how fallen it is. It is cold, 700° below zero, on some planets, while boiling and furiously hot, thousands of degrees Fahrenheit on others. I read history in the newspapers and see how fallen humanity is on this planet. But God has an eternal purpose for the redemption, the recreation, the rejuvenation, the deliverance of a creation that groans under the weight of the judgment that fell upon it because of sin.

Eternal redemption was in the mind of God from the ages past, and it reaches toward the unnamed ages that are yet to come. It leaps to the blasting of the seven trumpets, to the dreadful outpouring of the viles of wrath. It reaches to the vast consummation of the age. In this valley in which we live, between those two mighty peaks of eternity, God's redemptive program is pressed against our hearts. The Lord is saving sinners now. He is redeeming men and women now. It is the eternal purpose of God to deliver the world and to save those who find refuge in Jesus.

HE POURED OUT HIS OWN BLOOD

Look at one other thing. Our Lord enters beyond the veil into the Holy of Holies, bearing blood, not of bulls and goats, but pouring out His own blood in order to purge and to make atonement for our sins. The author of Hebrews illustrates this, beginning at 9:19,

> For when Moses had spoken every precept to all the people according to the law, he took the blood of calves and of goats, with water, and scarlet wool, and hyssop, and sprinkled both the book, and all the people,
>
> Saying, This is the blood of the testament which God hath enjoined unto you.
>
> Moreover he sprinkled with blood both the tabernacle, and all the vessels of the ministry.
>
> And almost all things are by the law purged with blood; and without shedding of blood is no remission.
>
> It was therefore necessary that the patterns of things in the heavens should be purified with these; but the heavenly things themselves with better sacrifices than these.
>
> For Christ is not entered into the holy places made with hands, which are the figures of the true; but into heaven itself, now to appear in the presence of God for us (Heb. 9:19–24).

Now that is the most startling thing I have ever read in the Bible! Is the author saying that the heaven of heavens is defiled? Is he saying that the inner sanctuary beyond the veil where God lives is defiled? That is what he is saying. When I think of it, I am so startled that I think he must not have understood. In the heaven of heavens, in the sanctuary of sanctuaries where God is, our Christ had to enter with blood of propitiation and atonement. Even the heavens are defiled! That is the place to which our prayers ascend; that is the place to which our praises go; but our prayers are imperfect and our praise, however we might strive to make it worthy, is not perfect. Our hearts, ascending into the sanctuary of God where His throne is, are not perfect. They are human and filled with imperfection. We cannot pray perfectly; we do not even know what we should ask. The Spirit has to make that intercession for us with groanings that we cannot utter.

The Entrance of Our Lord Beyond the Veil

How is the sanctuary of God to remain undefiled when sinful men and sinful women are entering into the presence of the holiness of God? Our Lord preceded us. He went into the sanctuary first with blood, propitiation, atonement, and forgiveness, and He cleanses the holy place even though we are there.

Nothing could be more vividly, theologically, and truthfully a presentation of that doctrine of the atoning blood of our Lord offered to God beyond the veil than this poem by Vachel Lindsay, one of the great poets of America. It was written upon the death of General William Booth, the founder and leader of the Salvation Army. It is entitled "General William Booth Enters Heaven."

Booth led boldly with his big bass drum,
Are you washed in the blood of the Lamb?
The saints smiled gravely and they said, "He's Come."
Are you washed in the blood of the Lamb?

Walking lepers followed rank on rank,
Lurching bravos from the ditches dank,
Drabs from the alleyways and drugfiends pale,
Minds still passion-ridden, soul-powers frail!
Vermin-eaten saints with moldy breath,
Unwashed legions with the ways of death,
Are you washed in the blood of the Lamb?

Every slum had sent its half-a-score
The round world over—and Booth had prayed for more.
Every banner that the wide world flies
Bloomed with glory and transcendent dyes.
Big-voiced lasses made their banjos bang!
Tranced, new born, they shouted and sang,
Are you washed in the blood of the Lamb?

Hallelujah! It was queer to see
Bullnecked convicts in that land made free.
Looms with bazoos blowing blare, blare, blare,
On, on, upward through the golden air,
Are you washed in the blood of the Lamb?

Booth died blind, but by faith he trod,
Eyes still dazzled by the ways of God.
Booth led boldly and he looked the chief:
Eagle countenance in sharp relief,
Beard a-flying, air of high command
Unabated in that holy land.

Jesus came out from the Courthouse door,
Stretched his hands above the passing poor,

The lame were straightened, withered limbs uncurled,
And blind eyes opened on a sweet new world.
Drabs and vixens in a flash made whole,
God was the weasel-head, the snout, the jowl;
Sages and sibyls now, and athletes lean!
Rulers of empires and of forests green!
The hosts were sandaled and their wings were fire!
Are you washed in the blood of the Lamb?
And their noise played havoc with the angel choir,
Are you washed in the blood of the Lamb?

Oh, shout Salvation! It was good to see
Kings and princes by the Lamb set free.
The banjos rattled and the tambourines
Jing-jing-jingled in the hands of queens.

And when Booth halted by the curb for prayer,
He saw his Master through the flag-filled air.
Christ came gently with a robe and a crown
For Booth the soldier while the throng knelt down.
He saw King Jesus—they were face to face,
And he knelt a-weeping in that holy place,
Are you washed in the blood of the Lamb?

That is what Christ did for us when He entered beyond the veil. How could we, sinful men and women, enter into that holy place where God lives? We enter under the blood of His atonement. We follow the prints of the feet of our blessed Lord. He goes before us. He prepares the way, and through the veil of His flesh rent in two, and in atoning grace and love preceding, He welcomes us also into the family of God and into the presence of the most holy One. There with Him, we rejoice and worship in an eternal salvation.

Oh, Lord, what a wonder, what an amazement, what an overwhelming realization! What God in Christ has done for us! We were separated because of sin, and now we are one in the atoning blood and grace and sacrifice of Jesus our Lord.

22

Our Sympathetic High Priest

Wherefore in all things it behooved him to be made like unto his brethren, that he might be a merciful and faithful high priest in things pertaining to God, to make reconciliation for the sins of the people.

For in that he himself hath suffered being tempted [*peirazō*], he is able to succor them that are tempted (Heb. 2:17–18).

For we have not an high priest which cannot be touched with the feeling of our infirmities; but was in all points tempted ["tried," *peirazō*] like as we are, yet without sin.

Let us therefore come boldly unto the throne of grace, that we may obtain mercy, and find grace to help in time of need (Heb. 4:15–16).

OUR NEED

We live in a world of sin, death, judgment, unhappiness, frustration, estrangement, misery, and disappointment. In fact, you could describe our earth as no better than a vast, illimitable cemetery in which we bury the dead.

Our needs rise to the heights of heaven and reach to the depths of our souls. We need a shepherd to guide us in the way and to show us how we may enter the gates of heaven. We need somebody to walk with us in this pilgrimage, for we are sojourners and wayfarers on this earth. We need someone who can encourage us and help us in our sorrows.

A woman came to the church saying, "Is there anyone here with a broken heart who can talk to me?" We need someone who can meet us in the hospital ward, who can stand by our side

197

before a newly-dug grave. We need someone who is not only moved by the heroic lives of the great martyrs, but someone who is also moved by the pitiful cries of the weak, the destitute, the poor, the unknown, the feeble, and the helpless. We need someone who can show us God and interpret to us the ways of the Lord.

There is an irrepressible longing in the heart of all mankind for God. That yearning hunger for the heavenly Father has inspired men to build temples in every land, to erect altars on every soil, and to consecrate a priesthood in every race and tribe of mankind. Whether it be in the refinements of modern civilization, the primeval forests of the long ago, the vast deserts of the nomadic tribes, or along the rivers of antiquity, that longing and hunger for God has ever been present and expressed.

One might say to us, "We can study nature and probe the secrets of science and find the hand of the great Creator." Others might say, "We can rise from nature up to nature's God." But in truth the ascent is too steep for our feeble climb. Somehow God must come down to us. We need a representative and an ambassador from heaven. We need a mediator between God and man.

We need someone who can reconcile us to the great God who made us—who can forgive our sins. The experience of sin is the darkest and ugliest fact in human life and experience. It plows up our hearts and homes. It separates us. It damns us. It condemns us. We are unable to escape its awesome and awful judgment. Who can deliver us? Who can save us both from ourselves and from the judgment of damnation? Who can keep us from falling into the fires of hell? Who can forgive our sins? Who can present us blameless and faultless before God? Who can open for us the gates of heaven? We need a great God and a great Savior who can deliver us from the judgment of sin and death.

CHRIST IS THE ANSWER FOR OUR NEEDS

All of the needs of the human heart and life are found in our great Savior and High Priest who is in heaven. He can teach us the ways of the Lord. He can show us God, for He is God Himself. "He that hath seen me hath seen the Father," Jesus said. If I want to know what God is like, I look at Jesus. If I want to know the ways of the Lord, I follow Jesus. If I receive the Lord, I receive Jesus. If I know God, I know Jesus. If I sit at the feet of Jesus, I sit at the feet of God. If I love Jesus, I love God. If I serve Jesus, I serve God. Jesus has come to show us the great, mighty, omnipotent God who made us.

Though I may not be able to pierce the mystery of the divinity, the deity, and the humanity as found in that one person, Jesus Christ, and though I may not be able to understand the unfathomable mystery of the Incarnation, I *can* receive the cup, brimming over with unmerited, undeserved love, favor, and grace that He offers to me from His nail-pierced hands. I can know God in Jesus our Lord.

Not only that, but we also find forgiveness of sin in Him. It is remarkable that no one in the earth has ever lived who is able to forgive our sins, to reconcile us to God, to die in our stead. Somehow, the heroic, the noble, and the famous are themselves just as much in need of substitution, propitiation, atonement, salvation, and forgiveness as we are. You can name the great of the earth—Alexander the Great, Caesar the Great, Charles the Great, Frederick the Great, Napoleon the Great. Yet it would never enter one's mind that even the most famous and heroic of all mankind could ever deliver us from the judgment of our sins.

But there is One who can, who did, and who does deliver us. "Who can forgive sins but God?" they asked in the New Testament. In order to demonstrate His power to forgive sins, at the word of His voice the dead lived again, the blind could see, the lepers were cleansed, the lame walked and rejoiced in God.

It is a remarkable thing that this Jesus who is so exalted and great bore the burden of the guilt of all mankind. He paid the entire debt that we owe to God for our sins.

You would think that one so exalted and mighty would be far removed from us, but instead He is one of us. He belongs to us. He is our brother. Jesus, the mighty God, the everlasting Father, is our Savior. As the ruler of the world, the earth, the sky, and the creation, Jesus presides over all history; yet He loves us. Underneath the vestments of His kingly garment is a heart that beats in sympathy for us. Our names are inscribed on the breastplate of our great High Priest. In His hands are the memorial marks of His redeemed and blood-bought family. He is one of us.

How many times do we fall into the mistaken persuasion that

maybe there was one point in history when the Lord assumed the form of a man, but that in His death and resurrection the man perished, and He returned to pure, spiritual deity in heaven. There is nothing concerning which the Bible takes more pains to declare and to present and to assure than that His recognitions are still human. He said, "Handle me, and see; for a spirit hath not flesh and bones, such as ye see me have" (Luke 24:39). He asked, "Do you have anything to eat?" And they gave Him a piece of a fish and a honeycomb, and He ate before them. And when they did not believe Him, He showed them the scars in His hands and feet and side.

There is no greater announcement than this: the God of all the universe is a man. The man who stood in Pilate's judgment hall and the man who lay dead in Joseph's new tomb is the same man who sits on the throne of God and is the Lord of all the earth. It is too good to be true.

CHRIST'S MEDIATORIAL MINISTRY IS EFFECTIVE NOW AND FOREVER

The tremendously effective ministry of the Lord as our great, sympathetic High Priest in heaven saves us now and forever. When He was on earth, He was not a priest. He was not of the tribe of Levi. Rather, He was of the tribe of Judah. He did not belong to the household of Aaron; He belonged to the household of David. When He came to the temple, He did not come to preside over the sacrifices or to burn incense. He came to teach the way of God when He came to the temple. But in the heavenly sanctuary in glory, He is our High Priest forever—not after the Aaronic order, but after the order of Melchizedek that endures through all generations and through all eternity. And as such, He is our sympathetic representative and mediator and intercessor in the sanctuary of heaven.

He does not throw us a bone like you would to a dog—a gesture of kindness or sympathy or tender-heartedness. He is rather moved by our infirmities. Our pitiful pleas and cries move His heart as they move one who would love us, care for us, remember us, and minister to us.

I have always thought that half of the cure of a patient is the sympathetic kindness of the attending physician. I can never forget, when I was sick, as a boy, the soft, tender hands of my mother. Jesus is like that—He is moved with the feeling of our infirmities. He does not overdrive the lame and the crippled among His flock. He carries the lamb in His bosom. He is our tender and precious High Priest, who is like one of us and is moved by our continuing needs.

Not only that, but also we are saved by his life in heaven. Sometimes I try to think through the profound, immeasurable meaning of Romans 5:10,

> For if, when we were enemies, we were reconciled to God by the death of his Son, much more, being reconciled, we shall be saved by his life.

We are saved by His life, that is, His life in heaven, His continuing life in glory. He keeps us saved.

The Christian experience is not historically isolated, as though we touched the Lord at one point in our lives when we were saved, regenerated, born again, and then at another point we have a dead, pulseless, and lifeless Savior. No! He lives to keep us saved. He lives to cleanse us. He lives to wash us. He lives to guide us and direct us. He is a living Lord.

Sometimes I think we as a people look at Jesus as if He were a picture in a stained glass window. He never steps out of the picture; He just remains there in that stained glass window. We look at Him on Sunday when we come to church, and we leave Him there. He does not live; He does not walk with us in the days of the week. We just see Him there in that window. Oh, no! Our Lord is a living Lord. He is never captured in just a picture or a crucifix or a symbol. Our Lord lives, and because He lives, we live with Him. He lives to keep us saved forever.

Look at the marvelous, beautiful words of Hebrews 7:25,

> Wherefore he is able to save them to the uttermost that come unto God by him, seeing he ever liveth to make intercession for them.

We live in this world, presided over by the prince who has the power of death. How do I know but that I will not fall into hell? What assurance do I have that I will ever be presented in the presence of God, redeemed, washed, cleansed, and saved? How do I know?

My assurance lies in the intercession of the Lord who lives forever. I am no match for Satan. We are not equal to him. Even Michael, when disputing with him about the body of Moses, dared not bring against him a railing accusation. If Michael, the archangel, dared not confront Satan, how could a poor, wretched worm made out of the dust of the earth confront him? That I would be able to overcome the sin and the wiles and the damnation of the devil is unthinkable. My assurance lies in the intercessory care and loving ministry of our Lord in heaven. He sends His angels to defend us. He surrounds us with His chariots of fire. It is He who saves us and preserves us and keeps us and ushers us some day into the presence of the great glory.

Could I parenthesize here for just a moment? The heart and the center of the Christian faith is not an organization or a system; it is a man. It is not a plan or a program; it is the man, Christ Jesus. Christianity is not a doctrine of forgiveness; it is somebody who forgives. Christianity is not a plan of salvation; it is somebody who saves us. Christianity is not a doctrine of substitution; Christianity is someone who loved me and gave Himself for me. Christianity is not a code of ethics or morality; it is the great glorious Lord who leads us into the ways of righteousness and holiness. Christianity is not a persuasion, a hope, a doctrine of immortality and life to come; Christianity is the picture you see in the baptismal service. We are dead with Him. We are buried with Him. In the grace and goodness of God we are raised to immortal life—eternal life in Him. That is the faith. It is a man, the man Christ Jesus. It is He who saves us, and it is He who keeps us saved.

He is presented here as being a loving and compassionate High Priest. Could anything be more beautiful?

> Wherefore in all things it behooved him to be made like unto his brethren, that he might be a merciful and faithful high priest in things pertaining to God, to make reconciliation for the sins of the people.
> For in that he himself hath suffered being tempted, he is able to succor them that are tempted (Heb. 2:17–18).

He is touched with our infirmities, and He is able to comfort and strengthen those who are tried. He is no different there in heaven than He was down here in this world in the days of His flesh. He was moved by the least cry.

Thronged on every side in a multitude, He stopped and asked, "Who touched Me?" Simon Peter said: "Lord, what an impossible question. You are pressed on every side, and yet you ask, 'Who touched Me?' " But Jesus said, "Somebody touched Me." A poor woman with an issue of blood had said in her heart, "If I can but touch the tassel on the hem of His garment, I will be saved."

In the days of His flesh, blind Bartimeus cried to the Lord, and all the people standing by said, "Hush, this great prophet from Nazareth has too many things to do to be bothered with you." Jesus stopped and said, "Bring him to Me." And He opened the eyes of the blind man.

While Jesus Himself was dying, a thief, crucified by His side, turned to the Lord and said, "When You come into your kingdom, could You remember me?" And the Lord replied, "This day you shall be with Me in paradise."

He was that way in the days of His flesh, and the author of Hebrews says that He is that way still. He is moved with the feelings of our infirmities. When anyone prays or cries, He bows down from heaven to hear and to see.

Can you imagine the great, mighty Lord God who stops to listen to the pleas and the cries of the least of His saints! "Whosoever shall call upon the name of the Lord shall be saved." He listens; He bows down His ear to hear when His people cry.

While I was in East Africa, one of the missionaries said to me, "Pastor, the tribe here could not pronounce the words 'Come By Me.' The nearest they could get to those English words were their words, 'Kum Ba Yah.' " That is what they sang— "Lord, Come By Me" or "Kum Ba Yah."

> Someone's cryin' Lord, kum ba yah!
> Someone's cryin' Lord, kum ba yah!
> Someone's cryin' Lord, kum ba yah!
> O, Lord, kum ba yah.